ADDING ADDICTION

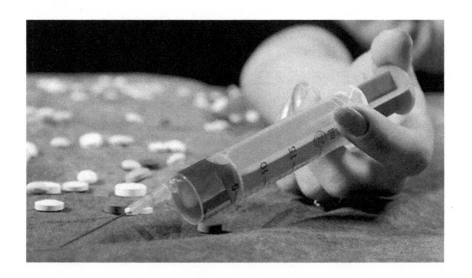

WRITTEN BY
THE ADDICT, FOR THE ADDICT

BRADLEY J. KORER

Adding Addiction

"Hi, My Name is Brad...
...And I Am an Addict"

Dedicated to those who've lost the battle to addiction

Table of Contents

I.

No PhD, But a Doctorate in Drugs

"THE INTRODUCTION"

I HAVE ALWAYS CONTEMPLATED THE reason street identifications for narcotics are names such as *Molly, Mary Jane, White Lady, Cid* and other human names. This way of classifying drugs is a bit ironic; drugs are like a person in your life. To be more specific, a significant other. Significant others have a relationship with a cohesive bond that people may think they understand, but there is ambiguity from an outsider's point of view (e.g. family and friends). In other words, no individual completely understands the bond except the two that are in the relationship. To be even more specific, drugs are like a relationship that is contaminated by domestic violence. As with domestic violence, if someone who is not directly involved in the relationship tries to claim they can comprehend the unhealthy partnership, they will feel the wrath from the submissive partner. The submissive partner will typically claim that you simply do not understand.

There are dangerously dominant and submissive roles played in these relationships. In a hypothetical scenario, your significant other is the dominant component of your relationship and has such a constricting hold of your collar that you are suffocating. (Take me literally or figuratively.) The significant other has authority and control, and dominates you in your daily routine. This relationship is as any other domestically violent human engagement: You never get into a relationship saying "This man or woman will degrade me, bring me down, and eventually beat me to a bloody pulp." You never

1

thought your true love could hinder or end your life; rather, you thought it enhanced your life. As time proceeds, you start to realize you depended on this person until they are the only reason why you are living. You cannot sleep, eat, or participate in any sense of happiness unless this partner is satisfied.

Parents, friends, loved ones, and family plead for you to break up with this person, and at first you ignore them. Your loved ones perceive this situation from an outside point of view; they clearly see what has blindfolded you. They continually ask why you are with this person. You start realizing where their point of view is spawning from, but as soon as you see the light, the dominant abuser persuades you that they simply do not understand. The abuser convinces you it is a unique relationship that you two can handle. You fall into this deceiving individual's trap. You comply with bogus information that fills your mind. This is because you have become dependent, and anything that proves your abuser's logic wrong you try to falsify. You begin making excuses to justify the wrongdoings. This abuse is progressively getting worse, and your life now revolves around the hardship the abuser inflicts on you. One night, you realize the abuser almost had you in serious trouble, got you arrested, or even nearly killed you.

You decide the next morning this is it; you are content with leaving this endangering nuisance in your life. Your brain is now seeing reality, and you are clearly grasping the situation placed before you. You slam the door until it nearly bursts off the hinges, but once you open the door to the heavenly light, the abuser grasps your arm and drags you back to rock bottom. Your friends and family tell you this person will kill you next time. You mentally respond, "Yeah...but I promise this was a one-time thing." You tell yourself this time you are taking control, proceeding to make justifications from any angle applicable. You lie to yourself in such a convincing way it somehow disguises the lie as an obvious truth. You are entering a vicious cycle that will soon be impossible to escape. For the time being, the abuser has apologized, and it seems to be better. As time continues, things are great between you and the abuser. That is, until one day the abuser commits a minor act of abuse – but it was only one hit; you can handle that.

"Oh, it was just a slip-up; Rome wasn't built in a day, right?"

The excuses continue, but you see them as logic and reason – not as excuses. Next time, the abuser strikes a little harder; the abuser beats you to the point that you cannot comprehend what happened. Although you swore to yourself this would never happen again, you rationalize the situation by convincing yourself that this time was different. The abuser was stressed financially, or with family, or with work, so this time it is "understandable." You continue to make excuses until you relapse to square one. This is the point at which you can consider yourself entering the brutal and vicious cycle of domestic violence.

You may be thinking to yourself, *I thought this book was about drugs, not domestic violence.* You are correct; the passage above is a metaphor. Read the entire section again and substitute "person" or "abuser" with the word drug(s) and the story would be identical. Refer back to my question, *"Why do we nickname drugs after humanlike names and characteristics?"* The ironic answer: with the power they have over addicts, they might as well be human. They will bring you down for years, ruin your life, deceive you until you do not possess a skin cell in contact with reality, but even though you consciously know this you cannot leave. You have been deceived by the drug, by yourself, and by your fantasy existence as a whole.

Slowly but surely, you are soon on an intensive search for the next level of "fantasy" (more commonly known as the "next high"), and you will not be satisfied until you have captured it. You make desperate attempts, deceive loved ones, and even endanger yourself. Your life now revolves around the drug; the drug is top priority. If you have encountered any domestic violence in your life, you can probably spot the similarities to drug abuse. You will inform everyone that everything is fine, that the drug is not hurting you and you have the situation under control. You will start making excuses like "I control my fate," "It is my life, back off," "I do not have an addictive personality," and, the most common, "No way that situation will happen to me." You can sit in the dark corner of your room pondering where things went wrong, who there is to blame, yet turn your head and ignore the catastrophe at hand and continue to place your affection with the drug. How did a normal human being with such an average or exceptionally promising life get to this point, and who is to blame for this misfortune?

People look to blame ghettos, certain races, or even certain countries. TV shows continuously portray cartels and the lower-class population as at fault for this drug crisis. People use them as scapegoats to mask the truth. As with many national crises, we blame the outside source rather than ourselves. For example, we seem to undermine what contribution the higher-class population, in fact the one percent, makes to the crisis. We completely ignore what the youth observe in this country from our adored role models. If it is the lower-class gangbangers' fault that our precious youth are developing meth scars, then why the hell does Lindsay Lohan look so strung out, and Heath Ledger is no longer breathing? Last time I checked, they were white and wealthy role models, and this is exactly where this "war on drugs" started. Not necessarily from the one percent, but from pointing our hypocritical fingers at the wrong places.

Be rational. If your upper-class city children are doing cocaine, I highly doubt they got the idea from someone in the underground cartel trails from Mexico. More than likely, they got the idea from 2 Chainz or Charlie Sheen. Charlie Sheen is now a known name for cocaine. The crisis partially started with millionaires living fantasy lives (because they obviously have the money), and then the kids of America perceiving it (let's keep blaming foreigners) and attempting to replicate the process (with the youth striving to live a similar lifestyle). Not many Americans can relate to the MS-13 drug cartels, but a hell of a lot of America relates to the media, Hollywood stars, and this type of lifestyle. This modern Hollywood lifestyle has three aspects: sexual attraction, acquired currency, and drugs.

Sexual desire is natural, and, frankly, needed for reproduction. Making money is known as the American Dream, and is entirely socially acceptable. These have been in the media and entertainment business since its origin, but what about drugs? Exactly how do drugs being thrown into the flashy lifestyle put the youth at risk of such a dreadful epidemic?

This lifestyle is projected from the media to the youth and throughout the country. Whether the politicians are doing Oxy and Percocet or a new pop artist produces a song about Molly, they contribute significantly to this issue. The media, your peers, and certain communities are the matchmakers in these metaphorical "domestic relationships."

Imagine the media and entertainment industry as the eHarmony matchmaker. It is widely known and reaches a plethora of people. It has an enormous impact that reaches individuals worldwide. The positive to this matchmaker (metaphorically) is that it does not have as strong of an impact on the individuals in the population. The song "Molly" has millions of views and is reaching a huge portion of our population, but it is not as persuasive as communities and individuals. This is why certain artists get aggravated when people blame them for certain controversial issues. The mass media and entertainment industry should not be blamed for single-handedly causing youth drug consumption, but it is something that is usually overlooked.

On the other hand, a community can be compared to a local chat line, one that has specific characteristics to reach the demographic it serves. It fits the style and charisma of the surrounding area. This matchmaker is designed specifically for a locality. For example, rich communities are aimed towards cocaine, while crack rocks are more common in poverty-stricken areas. If you want to prevent drug addiction, it is critical to understand what drugs are popular and being dispersed through your local community. Even though this matchmaker does not reach a large portion of people, there is a higher chance of the match being useful, or, in other words, influencing you into trying the drug.

If you have a child going to a rural party school, they are probably going to party more often than the child who went to an Ivy League school. It is solely based on the stigma of the campus. Many high school graduates attend "party schools" and end up party animals in college, while scholarly citizens go to Ivy League schools for the prestige. These two school types both have drug problems, as does the rest of America, but differ when it comes to the type of substance. For example, illegal Adderall use is probably more prevalent at an Ivy League institution than at most universities, but Molly and cocaine may be more prevalent at a smaller party school in the middle of nowhere. Adderall is used for those suffering from ADHD. If an individual consumes this amphetamine and does not have ADHD it may keep them up for hours on a focused study binge. Cocaine and Adderall are both drugs that make youth stay awake, either to party and consume copious amounts of alcohol, or to consume mass amounts of information. The point is these are both controlled substances, but the community sets who is being peer pressured to do which drugs.

The most powerful matchmaker is your peers; this is matchmaking that can be metaphorically a "group function." You are directly introduced to your future "abuser." In other words, your friends have accidently put you in the face of something that will, in time, ruin your life. For example, your friend introduces you to his/her co-worker. Your friend thinks the co-worker is a hard worker and an overall fun person to be around. They want you to ease up, and decide to set you and their colleague up on a date. After the date, you and the "friend" keep seeing one another, and eventually the relationship turns sour. It plummets into another case of domestic violence.

The peer pressure pertaining to substance usage plays out similarly to the situation above. Let's say your friend notices you have been stressed with school, and consequently wants to ease your mind. Your friend tried cocaine last weekend, and realized it really helps them let go for the night. Your friend is convinced that cocaine is fun, harmless, and overall would be great for you as a temporary fix. Your friend convinces you to do it, and you become a full-blown addict. Your friend obviously never meant for such a destructive relationship, but regardless, this is the outcome... Your friend just wanted you to have a sense of relief, not a life of despair.

I am not one to use a scapegoat in any way, shape, or form; in fact, you control your destiny. You are the ultimate product of the decisions you make in your life. Therefore, in a group function, people's ultimate being comes from people's decisions in life. People in your network have an influence that is much stronger than the media and entertainment industry. Keep in mind that most people who try drugs are young, therefore easily influenced. For the adults doing drugs, you are completely wrong if you think an average addict was forty-five years old and woke up on a Tuesday morning deciding to take a bump or two. They have been with their drug of choice for that long of a duration. It typically starts in childhood or adolescence, as with many iterations of domestic violence. It is all the individual knows and loves.

There are so many aspects of influence that it is hard to depict it to a science, but I can confidently say it can be broken down into micro, mezzo, and macro levels, those being peer influence, community influence, and of course the influence of the media and entertainment industry. With that said, I would never label the media, the community, or any one individual THE influence or the "scapegoat." These work as a team, although I do believe that friends influence one another with a greater impact than the other two aspects discussed above combined. Peers are often necessary to unlock the door to addiction.

There is a reason that there is a word just for this micro-level influence, the word every youngster hates – peer pressure. Peer pressure is very real and unfortunately very subconscious. No one can admit to peer pressure, because most of the time they have no idea they are being impacted by it. The commercials on television are a fluke; most fifteen-year-olds do not have the audacity to say, "You are only cool if you take a hit." Through all the times I have tried a drug, no one said anything close to that with a sense of seriousness. When the youth experiments with drugs, typically they walk the dark path with other close friends or family members. This is where people do not know they are peer pressuring.

With a smirk your girlfriend wants to sip on some whiskey, and obviously you do not want to be the only party pooper so you try it. Your girlfriend has now just successfully peer pressured you subconsciously. In a sense, ninety-nine percent of the time you are not even peer pressured solely by an individual; you are peer pressured by the deadly combination of an individual AND the situation. Honestly, if you never met an individual who consumed drugs, or were placed in a scenario where you were able to try it, how would you ever take your first dosage? You would not. In a hypothetical situation you call a friend, Joe Schmoe.

"Hey dude, what is happening tonight? My older brother left his bottle of whiskey here, and he left for school."
"Heck yes, let's do it!"

Curiosity kicks in, so the young individuals are pondering the situation. They know it is wrong, but after all, wrongdoing is humanity's natural vice.

"Okay Joe, you go first then I'll do it."
(Joe Schmoe kicks back a shot.)
"WOW, that was good, and now my body is all warm."

Joe Schmoe obviously decided to experiment, but what if it was just another night where the two kids played Xbox? This issue would never have come up in the first place. This was not the case. Every time the older brother was home from school, they got him to buy alcohol for them. He figured he was just being the cool older brother. Well, summer is over; where are the boys going to get their weekend fun? Once he leaves for school, Joe starts finding neighborhood citizens to contribute to an unknown addiction the boys are developing. My point is, what if that experimentation turns Joe into a hopeless alcoholic. Peer pressure alone cannot turn you into an addict, but it sure as hell can contribute. Even more bothersome, it can start it.

The aspect of peer pressure that is troubling is no one wants to confess that they are on either end of it, even if they know they are involved in the devilish game. It has such a negative connotation that if you are the person peer pressuring you are portrayed as the devil, and if you are on the receiving end you might as well be the devil's mindless sheep. The aspect of peer pressure that people have misunderstood is that the mindset of the participants is "If a friend is going down the wrong path, he wants to bring you with him." This is a false belief...why would anyone purposely go down a wrong path, or take a FRIEND down the wrong path? That is like saying my business went bankrupt, so now how am I going to make my best friend go bankrupt?

People doing drugs usually are young and free-spirited. With that said, they want their friend to "relax and live a little." No addict thinks, "I am going to destroy your life with this hit to satisfy myself." To the parents reading this book, be rational...we are talking about drug addicts, not psychopaths. It truly disgusts me that parents blame friends, and on top of that truly believe they are terrible people when they are simply just falling down a wrong path, similar to their child. This spawns from the fact that parents are in a state of delusion. They simply do not want to admit their child is a drug user because they put themselves in the situation to become one. This is problematic, since the first step in recovery is admitting. How can an adolescent admit to their start of addiction if their parents convince them it is someone else's fault?

Another tricky aspect that parents ignore is the fact that it's not as simple as, let's say, playing catch (with a giver and receiver); it is more complex than that. Parents have this perception of their dear children being incapable of losing their innocence. The parents' rationalizations work overtime to spawn the idea of blaming someone else. "This must be the friend's fault, because my kid would never be so irrational and ignorant." This thought is usually mutually held by both parents, so what does that tell you? It should inform you that a large part of peer-pressure situations boils down to "I'll do it if you do it." So, in that case, who is to blame? Is it the individual who stated that, or the person who did it first? The fact of the matter is; friends give off a sense of protection. In other words, no harm. A friend would never put you in danger, but when it comes to the abuse of substances and danger, there is no connection linking them.

Once again, peer pressure is subconscious most of the time. A youngster is usually peer pressured by the situation, or the series of events. Joe's brother was out of town, the brother left whiskey. Joe and his friend had curiosity. Joe tried it first to look cool, and then months later became an alcoholic. This is a realistic representation of peer pressure, not "take this hit, or else you're a chicken." Friends typically get into trouble together. With that said, friends never want to put you in danger, and they do not feel they are most of the time. This is why people are unaware when they participate in peer pressure.

Whether the view is right or wrong, your perception is your reality. If you truly believe the drugs are causing no harm, then it is your reality. This is why I call it a falsified reality. You and the drugs are a duo causing this falsified life. The drugs give you a sense of carelessness, and you yourself lose grasp of the fact that every milligram you put into your body is slowly decaying your well-being. This duo is detrimental to your health.

I do not feel sympathy to addicts necessarily, but I do give empathy. People must realize no one wants to be a "deadbeat" drug addict. People need to realize that when addicts start, it is similar to how everyone experiments with a little puff of marijuana in an innocent childhood life. The difference is when an addict drinks the first sip, smokes the first puff, or sniffs the first line, they spiral into the pit, to eventually slam into rock bottom. The only way to come to an understanding of this fantasy life the addict is living is to be rational enough to depict your situation as it stands, or, more common than not, have a tragic event take place. You must be able to take off the deadbolted blindfold or else plunge head first to your rock bottom. Essentially, this is my personal perception of drugs.

They will lead you to three places: hospitals, incarceration, and/or death. I have personally been to two of the three, and I have never been incarcerated.

I am not a hypocrite, and I am not going to say drugs are pointless. This is the only book that advocates sobriety that will be this sincere, truthful, and, simply, as real as it gets. Why would anyone do something as expensive and stupid as drugs if they were pointless? In fact, they are a blast; they are an adult Disneyland – a real time of euphoria. They bring joy and, while doing that, they diminish the hardship that life brings. They literally interact with the mind to enhance and decrease certain neurotransmitters and receptors in your brain such as serotonin and dopamine. You can take something such as Xanax to forget, something like cocaine to be alert, and something like LSD to be in a parallel universe. Essentially, a junky can feel any way they want, and feel that way on any day at any time. Any obstacle that is thrown your way, you do not have to beat. You can just simply ignore it and be content. You can live a life free of drama, you can believe you are the smartest person in the world, and you can build the confidence to feel you can do anything you want to. But there are two issues with living life like this. For starters, it is only masking your issues, not fixing them. Secondly, it only takes time before this joy and wonder comes to a screeching halt.

So, who am I to understand drugs so well? You probably have me figured out – I am a rich, old, and gray psychiatrist who has never snorted, smoked, or ingested a chemical in my life. I am just another old man preaching about how bad drugs are, so I can receive my weekly pay and royalties on book sales. Well, if you believe that, you are sincerely wrong, my friend. I am no PhD. Although I have not obtained a PhD, I faced it firsthand when I was on my almost eighteen-month-long binge that nearly led me to my tombstone. When I was in rehabilitation, the people who influenced me the most were the people who have accepted the lifelong challenge to recovery, and were now living a virtuous life, paying their knowledge forward. The old man with a PhD obviously knows what he is talking about, although it is merely education and not practical action. It is science, not comprehending emotion.

This book faces the overlooked complexity of addiction. The war on drugs is inefficient and is a waste of taxpayer's money, because our basic solutions and explanations are insufficient regarding something as complex as addiction. We dumb it down to such an extreme that most of America has the mindset of "drug abusers are losers, simple as that." I can confidently say I have been more mind-altered, addicted, and intoxicated than anyone reading this. This is something I am not ashamed of, nor proud. I am now an advisor of a national organization, have received a bachelor's degree in business, am a stakeholder with a multi-million-dollar E-commerce company, am working on numerous projects, and am confident that I am the furthest thing from a loser…but I am still a recovering ADDICT.

This is me; I am Brad Korer, a recovering addict for life. I have received a second chance, and it was for one reason: to publish my story. This is my story to challenge the misconceptions and inefficiency of both rehabilitative treatment programs and society as a whole. I had read many stories such as mine while on drugs, and I can honestly come to the conclusion that it did not work…I needed a story of my own. I see those addicted to drugs right now laughing just as I did, ignorantly thinking, "This kid's an idiot, I got my shit under control." If you are that person, your domestic partner just grabbed your leash and viciously yanked on it.

I did not write this to be judgmental, nor to have written a sob story for myself. I published this for one reason, and one reason only – to demonstrate what can and will inevitably happen to those who have the domestic drug collar on so tight that when it tightens you will suffocate. I want addicts out there to know that I understand what it is like living a life with the addictive personality. I understand that your struggle is not as simple as people perceive it to be, and the issues you have developed blossomed over a long and complex process. I have written this book to enlighten the youth so no one has to deal with the hardship my metaphorical "abusers" brought me to. Will it work? If you let it. I am not here to give you the twelve steps we have been using for decades, I am not here to be your PhD savior, and I am not here to push other programs that are completely outdated. I am here to be me, the addict that has figured out how to live with the addictive personality.

"Hi, my name is Brad, and I am an addict."

II.

The Loss of Innocence

"THE EXPLANATION"

USE A PHILOSOPHICAL APPROACH WITH THIS question: what is innocence?

The definition of innocence:

A. Freedom from guilt or sin through being unacquainted with evil: blamelessness.
B. Chastity.
C. Freedom from legal guilt of a particular crime or offense.

Who determines innocence from guilt?
Would you consider the tooth fairy tale innocent or a sinful lie?

See, before understanding a drug addict, you must understand innocence. When the youth is innocent, you may compare them to a baby, learning every move their caregiver is making. The adolescent is observing the world around them, as they did with their caregiver. When I say youth, I'm including the fourteen-, fifteen-, or even eighteen-year-old. Innocence could be defined as being un-ashamed. This leads us to our next question: what makes us ashamed of our actions? This answer is simple: "knowing what is socially acceptable." Acceptability can vary between localities, ages, and personal mindsets. For example, it is a sin to eat ham with cheese on it according to the Hebrew faith, but in a Catholic church this is a delightful after-service snack. This is exactly what I mean by what is socially acceptable, and how much it can fluctuate.

Is it acceptable for a six-year-old to say, "That teacher gave me a D-minus, what a b****"? Absolutely not. Is it socially acceptable for someone in high school to say that? I heard it on a daily basis... So how does this innocence transformation happen? When you reach seventeen and three quarters, do you have the right to speak so explicitly? Obviously, that is not how life works. When cursing becomes socially acceptable, it builds a sense of innocence to certain populations. Once again, this may vary depending on area, age, personal values, and the situation. An eleven-year-old at church in a conservative town would be forbidden to use any form of explicit language. An eleven-year-old in Compton or South Central may not receive any criticism for using foul-mouthed language. As for most issues regarding the loss of innocence, they are not as extreme as the ones I just listed, so here is a more realistic hypothetical situation.

Frank was a young child who was raised in an average middle-class family in Washington, D.C. Frank and his friend watched a movie that must have ducked under the parents' radar. In this crime-filled movie a cop told a villain, "I got you now, bastard." Frank was not capable of saying this, because he knew that must be what his mom called having "a potty mouth." Frank's friend, on the other hand, experimented with his first attempt at cursing; he called the school bully a bastard. Frank was in disbelief; he would never expect his friend to use such foul-mouthed language. He confronted his friend, and his friend responded, "Frank, grow up and stop being a baby." Frank became indecisive, confused, and offended.

Frank decided that he was not going to surround himself with such a bad influence. Frank did not hang out with his buddy for a couple months, but eventually decided to give his friend one more chance. He invited him over to play a game of their imaginary "Batman." They went to the park, because it happened to be the best place to play this imaginary game due to the high jungle gym that reminded them of a tower in Gotham city. The two boys met another young kid named Cody. Cody was known as the cool kid on the playground, because his older brother was always at the skate park right next to it. When Cody was informed that he was going to have to be the arch nemesis while the other boys were Batman, he said, "Why, that is bulls**t!" Frank's mind told him this was clearly inappropriate behavior, but he kept a mental note and decided to continue his game without further action. He was quite uncomfortable, but he controlled his impulse to say something as he beat out this nerve-racking moment.

Frank is now thirteen years old, and he is seeing a "girlfriend" at school. His little crush seems saddened, and he asks what is wrong. She informs him, "I do not get the math we are learning, and my mom is being a b**** about it."

"Wow," Frank thinks in his head. "My friend is cursing and now my girlfriend is too." There is a moment of silence, and then Frank responds, "Well, that is f**ked up."

There is the ticket! The loss of innocence has happened through this complex and drawn-out process. Now refer back to the first chapter and how peer pressure typically spawns. Was it spawned by the individual or by the situation? Even though this level of deviance is extremely miniscule, this example is identical to every other deviant action. Instead of "cursing," substitute "having sex," "lying," "fighting," and, of course, "using drugs." The fact of the matter is, most wrong-doings typically arise out of this same scenario.

From the time a child enters school, they are learning corruptive actions. The child is no longer influenced solely by their caregiver. They have now entered into an inevitable phenomenon, watching and interpreting the world change around them. Friends are transferring from watching Barney, Batman, and Barbie to watching Teen Nick and Adult Swim. They are no longer listening to Disney tracks; they are listening to what the "older" and "cool" kids are listening to. Even looks are changing; wearing Power Rangers and superhero outfits is no longer cool. The youth is now developing specific fashions, phases, and scenes to differentiate themselves. Their cliques and groups are developing. Goth, nerds, gamers, skaters, and several other groups are emerging. Through generations one stereotype has remained consistent, which is the rebel, the outlaw, the non-conformist. What is so appealing about this? Wrongdoing has always been the human vice.

Could you imagine the typical group of twelve-year-olds doing cocaine? That is highly doubtful. Do not misconstrue this; they are still experimenting with wrongdoing. A twelve-year-old is more likely to, let's say, sneak out. As with the cussing example, the first time a friend does it it's a deviance in the youth's perception, but two years later is it seen as acceptable. Now sneaking out is no longer shameful, or is almost, in a sense, an innocent action in the eyes of the youth. Half the school is now sneaking out so it is no longer deviant behavior.

Now let's say the new deviance is sex. The first girl in the eighth grade to have sex is now known as a big slut throughout the entire campus. Why is this? This is because it is socially unacceptable to have sexual intercourse at this age. As this young girl's friends hear her stories of how wonderful sex is, they decide to try it. In a couple years, sex is so common it no longer has a negative connotation. Once again, it transforms to an innocent action. The trend is identical with most youth deviances. With that said, here comes the new sinful action: puffing on cigarettes. This typically has a similar story...hopefully you see the phenomenon that most people overlook. This trend is the fact that youth only sees deviance where there are limited participants, and once the number of participants increases, the sense of innocence takes a positive correlation.

A year later, marijuana is now the act children participate in. This also plays out identically to the other deviance situations. There is a slight difference here, because this is the opportunity for addicts to get the green light on the dangerous road of addiction. Sex can lead you to pregnancy or sex addiction, cigarettes can lead to cancer or chronic cigarette smoking, and, last but not least, substances can lead to drug addiction (which usually starts with marijuana). I beg all of you reading this: do not misinterpret my words. I do not believe a marijuana smoker needs to be sent straight to an intensive in-house rehabilitation center the moment they take the first puff; that is thinking irrationally. Let us be honest – over half of the people reading this have tried marijuana; even our current president (Obama) has admitted to prior usage. The primary reason I am even including marijuana in this book is the fact that it's widely known and accepted as the gateway drug.

What does this entail? It is obviously in a different category than meth or heroin. We have separate sentencing by law, we have different conceptions about it, and many political figures argue that marijuana should be legal when no one in their right mind would fight for legalization of meth. Marijuana has been proven to be nearly harmless, natural, and non-addictive (at least chemically). I am not stating that I support, or do not support, the legalization of marijuana. I am merely stating facts. So why is it a big deal? It is known as the key needed to unlock addiction. This is the first high that could potentially lead to that restless search for the next one.

Marijuana typically is the differentiation point between the drug addict and the occasional or habitual marijuana smokers. The majority of youths and their network of friends are satisfied with marijuana smoking, and that is where their experimenting typically starts and ends (usually late teens/early twenties). The other people and networks plunge into something that they could never imagine happening. The network wanders into a new level of substances, and they viciously get their innocence snatched from them before they even have a chance to make contact with it again. Where does it end? For most of humanity's population it ends approximately after the late teenage years through the early twenties, but what about the ones who have fallen in love with their poison of choice? How does this phenomenon happen...? Believe it or not, the same way that Frank's cussing did. That is, first standing behind your conviction, then taking a mental note when it becomes more common, until the behavior is so common it now seems socially acceptable.

This may be hard to grasp, but areas and social establishments have made it socially acceptable to consume narcotics. For example, a university with alcohol and party drugs. This has an aroma of comfort, and almost that sense of innocence about doing the substances. You may ask yourself how the hell usage of drugs is innocent, but it is because they are seen as a socially acceptable behavior (at least by the micro-level population an individual might be in).

The point of this section is to further demonstrate the complexity of a brewing addiction. With the above information, you can infer that the youth has been experimenting with deviance since a small child. Deviance is what contradicts what is socially acceptable. Once again, what is socially acceptable can be determined by age, location, gender, culture, and even the particular situation at hand. Actions can become socially acceptable if the population confers a sense of innocence on them, which correlates with the amount of participants in a given network. With that said, if the population finds it acceptable to do drugs, it is highly probable you will find it acceptable as well.

Unfortunately for addicts, they surround themselves with other addicts or drug users; consequently, it becomes innocent and acceptable. Until you completely comprehend an addict's point of view, you cannot understand why they are doing it. I believe it is a necessity to understand what the green light is to enter the dark road. The biggest aspects to comprehend from this section are deviance, what is socially acceptable, and what innocence truly entails. If what you are doing is socially accepted by the population you are in then you see it as acceptable, therefore not deviant. If it is not deviant, then you see this action as innocent (therefore you do not see the harm). This is precisely how a drug addict starts his or her path.

"MY TRANSFER FROM INNOCENCE"

MY PERSONAL STORY STARTS WITH freedom. My father told me, "With freedom comes responsibility." This is definitely a cliché, although this sentence is powerful. As an adolescent, you gain more freedom. Consequently, you must be responsible with the freedom you are given. The idea is to take the freedom and do what you know to be right. What is right, or not shameful? Once again, what is socially acceptable dictates what is "innocent." These are words that stuck with me for some while; at least, until peer pressure altered what I found to be socially acceptable.

My start to childhood freedom came after we moved out of the terrifying slums of North Las Vegas. Growing up in Las Vegas was rough on a young child. The violence, the hospital trips, and the plethora of drug/gun cartels put many bystanders at risk—including my family. Before I knew it my peers started using drugs and alcohol. Right then I declared sobriety for the rest of my life. I was made fearful by the information my parents and local programs like D.A.R.E. gave me. These channels of communication rightfully convinced me that drugs were not acceptable and were extremely dangerous. With that said, I never decided to partake in wrong-doings in Las Vegas. I was mostly concerned for my safety rather than fitting in, and so was my father.

My father sold his profitable printing business located outside the Vegas strip and moved us out of Northern Las Vegas in order to flee the crime, insanity, and drugs. Ironically, my dad moved us to where I would start experimenting with the deceitful actions that I observed, although refrained from doing, in "Sin City." My freedom blossomed after fleeing the danger of Las Vegas to a beautiful middle-class

Virginia neighborhood. The reason I'd had limited freedom beforehand was the safety hazards the pits of Vegas contained.

My freedom was spawned when we moved to Ridge Run, Virginia. More specifically, my freedom started with my father's permission to go to my girlfriend's house by myself. In the eighth grade, I met my first "real" girlfriend, Kylie. We were in the typical state of puppy love, and we would tell people marriage would be waiting for us at the age of eighteen. It got to a point that I would leave my house at noon and not come back till late that night, which my father was content with.

Kylie and I were dating for some time, doing typical childhood activities, including: swimming, bike riding, and daily 7-Eleven runs. During the weekends, we would be with one another till curfew, which was at 10:00 p.m. We were truly living the typical middle-class childhood life that I had never experienced in Las Vegas. Her parents loved me, and my parents felt the same about her family. We were great children who thoroughly enjoyed each other's presence. You can call this the state of innocence. The ignorance of the deviant acts in our middle-school community temporarily blinded us, but this state of innocence was not permanent.

It started to change at a very vast rate. The first sign of deception came during the eighth grade summer. I was sneaking out for sexual pleasure, but thinking it would be terrible to actually have intercourse. Having "real sex" was so wrong at the time, I was afraid of what people would think of us. This refers back to what is socially acceptable, and for a thirteen-year-old making out is acceptable, according to the perception of that age group. On the other hand, intercourse would be so socially unacceptable I could not even consider it. I would have thoughts about having intercourse, but I knew that was the devil speaking on my shoulder.

On the other hand, sneaking out was not the devil hollering in my ear...I did not see this as a guilty action, because it was socially acceptable in the eyes of the eighth-grade population. I was never caught, so I saw no harm in what I was doing. I never thought about the consequences, therefore I never internalized why my father said to be in at 10:00 p.m. and stay in. I figured he still wanted to assure himself he was in control. I was naïve about the possibility that I could be arrested, robbed, kidnapped, or get into trouble. All I figured was he was my father, so he had to address his authority as such.

The deviance I was participating in was not deviant to me or my school's population. It was only deviant in the eyes of the adult demographic, but pish-posh, what do they know. My point is, I was turning rebellious subconsciously, but in my mind Kylie and I were not doing drugs or having intercourse. We were two innocent youngsters that were simply "growing up."

We were not innocent by any means; in fact, I even started sneaking into her house when her parents were not home during the summertime. Kylie was cool with that, and saw it as perfectly acceptable. All her friends did it, and they were all good kids in her parent's eyes. We figured as long as it was not harming her parents, what harm was it causing at all? If our parents never found out, then we could not have been too rebellious. We were under the parents' radar due to the fact that I would leave before they got home from their daily ritualized lives, and come back when they returned to their residence with no suspicion that I'd been there beforehand. Even in the situations of "close calls" (e.g. parents coming home early from work or Kylie's older brother coming home, etc.), I would hide in closets or depart the residence through the window.

My father was being fooled as well; I simply told him Kylie's mom was home. The trust I had built with my dad was the foundation of never being caught. I had instilled so much trust in my father through deceiving him. It was now at the point where I was sneaking out several times per week. This gave me the ability to go from the "inch" to the "yard." If you are asking what this has to do with drug addiction, remember the complexity, and how early the loss of innocence truly starts.

I continued playing these deceitful games until I found out the heartbreaking news that Kylie was smoking cigarettes. I even contemplated breaking up with her. I decided not to, just because my mother smoked cigarettes. This was partially socially acceptable to me, therefore was, in a sense, not associated with guilt...well, not much at least. The other part of me referenced my population, and what they saw as acceptable. In the eighth grade, smoking anything is probably looked down upon by the youth's population, especially in our middle-class town of Ridge Run. I was stuck between a rock and a hard place; I was not sure if this was acceptable or not. On a less meaningful and personal level, the smell of the cigarette smoke clenched my stomach, causing a woozy feeling in my body every time we kissed, although after some time I became immune to it. The cigarettes soon became benign in our relationship, because it became a part of the puppy-love relationship.

On a random night weeks after Kylie had started smoking, curiosity spawned in my mind about cigarettes, and I consistently contemplated trying them throughout the night. The idea of doing something I knew was wrong seemed so cool. Although temptation was optimal, I decided against it. I knew my dad would kill me if he smelled the nasty ashtray aroma on my clothes. Not only was the fear of my father a restraint between me and the cigarette, but also, at this point, not many people were smoking cigarettes. I was in a battle over whether it was okay to do, but, like I said, I surrendered to my curiosity.

One night, I was smooching on Kylie and smelled a smoky aroma, but it was not cigarettes. The scent was much more herbal and fruity than that of a cigarette. It was a smell I had not encountered since I had left North Las Vegas. Although I was not sure what the smell was, I instantly knew it was not a cigarette. The fact that it had a smooth, almost fruity smell, baffled me. It was concrete evidence that the aroma did not originate from a Camel smooth. Even though it smelled better than a cigarette, the aroma was much more present and powerful. In fact, I had smelled it upon entering her block. I figured it was a skunk in the woods that were located a couple miles west. They were everywhere during the summertime.

I met Kylie on her front stoop when the smell viciously bombarded my nasal cavity. When we proceeded into the house, I noticed her eyes were bloodshot, and I was obviously naïve about the situation, believing her blatant lies, which she already had premeditated. She told me she'd started smoking a new brand of cigarettes, and her eyes had an "adverse reaction" to it. "Whatever that means," I thought to myself. Her answers were odd, not because of what she said, but because of how programmed and ready she was to be questioned about it. She had never lied to me before, so I believed her false statements, similar to how my father believed mine. Young, naïve, and dumb, I had no reason to be skeptical of anything. I figured the only reason I was a little skeptical was I had never smelled such a good-smelling cigarette. But, in reality, the only cigarette I'd smelled was the Camel smooth she preferred and the Virginia Slims my mother smoked.

The incident cleared from my mind, and I didn't give it much thought after believing the blatant lies. Two days later, we decided to go to a local water park. As we were leaving out the door Kylie asked, "Brad, could you run upstairs and grab my purse and bathing suit?" I saw her purse, but I could not find her swimming bottoms. I went in her purse to see if her bathing suit had already been put in her bag, and I discovered that she hadn't changed her brand of cigarettes. The identical Camels made me ponder, but as a young adolescent I did not think much of it at the time. This did not necessarily give me reason to call her a liar (knowing the little I did at that age), but it did leave a plethora of unanswered questions. I decided to ask my good friend Marcus about it. I felt Marcus could possibly give me information to clear up all of this confusion.

Marcus was my best friend growing up through middle school and the earlier years of high school. He also lived close to my girlfriend. On weekend nights when I would want to hang out with Kylie, I would stay at Marcus's house. Here is another prime example of peer pressure. If Marcus complied with sneaking out, but I convinced him to sneak out to Kylie's, whose fault was it…? *(Just a little food for thought.)*

Regardless, Marcus and I were quite the masterminds of sneaking out. One hot summer night, we discreetly snuck out in the midst of the night, directly out of Marcus's back door. I proceeded to text Kylie once we were outside to come down and join the party. Once we got there, it seemed her and her friend Shay had started a party of their own, smoking her "newly preferred cigarettes." Being thirteen, I was very ignorant regarding the situation before me...I literally sat there and talked to them thinking this was one really strong cigarette.

You've probably figured out from my description that this was not tobacco; it was marijuana. I noticed as she was smoking this "new type of cigarette" that she was acting very weird. She was continually repeating herself, laughing in a psychotic fashion, thinking abnormally abstractly, and showing other behaviors I had never seen from her before. Let me tell you that this hit of reality was a slap in the face that made my head do spins at a full 360 degrees. I could not grasp the fact that my girlfriend was doing drugs. Keep in mind that at this time marijuana was far from acceptable. Essentially, it was not an act of purity – it was deviant on the grounds of what was socially acceptable for our particular demographic.

The first semester-long anti-substance abuse courses originate around this age. The course's primary purpose is to warn you of the inevitable consequences of drugs, and I could not believe my girlfriend was ignoring all of those lessons. She was deceiving our peers, elders, and society as a whole. The fact of the matter was, this behavior was not socially acceptable and was considered extremely deviant by our population. The only people who seemed to feel I was overreacting were the friends with older siblings, such as Marcus. This is not coincidental. The youth with older siblings see behaviors such as this as more acceptable; essentially they have already seen and accepted this deviant behavior. It would be an interesting study to see if having older siblings correlates to drug usage.

Like I said, Marcus was not surprised whatsoever, but I was downright outraged. I flipped Kylie off and sprinted back home as fast as my feet would take me. I went home and cried my eyes out.

"I know sneaking out was something my father said not to do, but everyone did it... My dad is just the stupid one, but smoking marijuana is illegal!" I sighed at Marcus.

"I don't know, man, my brother and all of his friends got caught smoking pot last week, and he told my mom everyone does it. He was just experimenting. He swore on his life."

I was so baffled; I didn't know anyone that would find this acceptable...well, except Marcus, I guess. Now, keep in mind what is socially acceptable at certain ages. Marcus did not see the point of worrying about a relationship so miniscule, although he also felt it was not necessary to explore his curiosity about marijuana's effects. Marcus was probably at that "mental note" stage. Recall the cursing example – the first time the child heard a curse word, he said something. The second time, he just took a mental note. Since the child has heard the word before, it becomes less deviant. For most deviant actions, it becomes less shameful the more we see it. A good example is speeding. We see it so much that it is almost not "deviant" at all. Marcus had seen his brother smoke. Consequently, when he saw Kylie stoned, it was not as shocking.

Marcus and I no longer talked to Kylie and her whole deceitful clan, per my request. I requested this on the grounds that they were so deviant from our eighth-grade population, and I did not want to be associated with them. Marcus agreed. Months went by of Kylie begging for me back, and she swore she would quit smoking. She even claimed she would cut Shay loose as a friend. I finally gave in to her, and we were considered a couple once again. Everything was fine for a while. In fact, she fulfilled her promise and quit talking to Shay for a couple months. We were back into a daily routine of swimming, bike riding, and playing neighborhood games. It was a time of rejoicing, and I was happier than ever to feel normal in our prospering relationship.

I became very close with her neighborhood friends. Sarah, Megan, Donald, and Will would always come over and hang out with us. We were now living the typical youngster life. Will was part of our chess club, and Sarah and Megan were both cheerleaders who typically kept out of trouble. All three of them were wonderful middle-class citizens with promising futures. Donald, on the other hand, was fleeing a life that was essentially set out for failure. His mind was corrupted as a young boy by a gang we will not name in this book (for security purposes). Donald's family fled the northern part of the state with similar reasoning to my father's: to promise Donald a life he could not obtain in his previous habitat of violence, danger, and drugs. Donald adapted to the average American environment quickly, although we knew he did smoke marijuana somewhat habitually. We did not mind due to the fact that he didn't smoke *too* much, and when he did it was at his house with his brother.

Donald was not the only one bringing around the marijuana aroma, though. Kylie seemed to be back on the bandwagon. This time, her excuse was that she went to Shay's and she was just around the smoking. I was not a person to blame for association, or to force someone to not hang out with another person because of their actions. I was fine with Shay hanging around again, but not with Kylie participating in the festivities. Regardless, I did not believe her, due to the fact that the aroma smelled as if she was wearing marijuana perfume. What made me significantly indecisive was that this time her eyes were clear as day. Maybe she was telling the truth, but the smell continued to be on her several days of the week... I was extremely confused. Her attitude was once again significantly changing, but I could not grasp whether she was lying about the marijuana smoking or not.

The week before we entered high school, Marcus, Kylie, Donald, and I were swimming. Her parents had just customized a beautiful deck with flowers surrounding the circumference of her yard. As we were getting ready for our typical summer fun of enjoying the swimming pool and the other luxurious additions, I got the answer that I had been seeking relentlessly regarding Kylie's marijuana consumption or lack thereof. It only took this one statement for me to slam my cup on Kylie's newly built deck and walk out her door for the final time.

Donald said, "Damn, them buds got me baked yesterday."

This time, I was so filled with anger. So many hurtful things were said, but I saw this as a big deal. Marcus also confessed that he smoked with them, making it even worse. I was so self-conflicted and confused that I emotionally just shut down.

I was so distraught. I was watching the world change, thinking it was spiraling into hell and that Jesus's resurrection was soon to be undergoing its process. You are probably in disbelief that I, the addict who nearly died, was in shock that his friends were losing their innocence to substances. I started noticing that more childhood friends were experimenting with marijuana, but I personally refused for months on end. Like they say, curiosity killed the cat...and I thought to myself, "I refuse to be the dead cat."

Regardless of my strong run with sobriety, one night my curiosity finally got the best of me. I couldn't help but wonder what was so magnificent about smoking marijuana, and I decided I would find out firsthand. With my hands shaking and heart racing, I took my first puff. I was hesitant and very nervous, but went through with it, similar to Frank and his first encounter with cursing. Smoke was rising out of Marcus's shed and in and out of my mouth while I impatiently waited for the outcome.

My head was looking around rapidly when I said, "Dude, this is dumb. I do not feel anything."

Marcus then told me with a smirk to hit the bowl a little harder. He said I must inhale as if I were drinking through a straw. I figured I had gone this far against my morals, so I might as well experience the effects. I viscously inhaled the toxins as hard as I could till I coughed like a fifty-five-year-old alcoholic that smokes a pack a day. My shoulders were at ease, my mind was thinking abnormally abstractly, and I was laughing hysterically. I started to realize why Kylie just let loose and was so careless when she was stoned. Something terrible happened: I actually loved it. The future addict had now taken his first puff. To think I took this one hit and the next day I was doing methamphetamines is not realistic, but it sure as hell started me down the path.

I did start using marijuana in a more habitual matter. I was smoking every weekend. I was now in the group labeled "pot-heads." I had fallen into this situational peer pressure, listening to music that advocated marijuana smoking, and even dressing in Rastafarian colors. I felt more accepted by my network of friends. We were smoking every Friday and Saturday night as soon as Marcus's mom fell asleep. A couple of other friends started joining our clique and smoking marijuana with us. You could consider us the small and deviant clique of the eighth and ninth grade. Some looked up to us as rebellious, some looked down on us as losers, but everyone knew who we were and what we did. We loved it.

Friday at 3:30 p.m., the bell that everyone was anticipating would ring. Some went to sporting events, other went to clubs, and we went to go put ourselves in a state of euphoria from the pot smoke. In theninth grade, it got to the point where Marcus and I were tired of being portrayed as pot smokers who did nothing to contribute to our school, and we decided to try out for the school's lacrosse team. We thought we were the only two who smoked on the entire team, therefore we kept it on the down-low. This once again goes back to what is socially acceptable. We did not want the team knowing that we smoked if it seemed too deviant for that particular population of athletes. We practiced Monday through Thursday, and participated in our other hobby of smoking reefer on the weekend. We had our two lives pretty balanced out, keeping them separate and distinguished from one another. Marcus and I started getting along with many team members; one of them in particular became a very close friend.

Jayden Powers, a midfielder on our lacrosse team, became close to Marcus and me. He also participated in our alter-ego lives. He had smoked marijuana before we all met, but once we met, he was instantly an addition to our circle. Jayden and I had a stronger bond than the rest of our circle of friends. In fact, we eventually became best friends as Marcus kind of drifted off to alternate activities and friends that consumed his time.

As time went on, Marcus skipped lacrosse practice, causing the team to start disapproving of him. With that said, Jayden and I drifted away from Marcus slowly but surely, day after day. He eventually quit the team without telling anyone. This directly resulted in Jayden and me developing a relationship that continually grew stronger. We had now become best friends. Jayden had his own network of buddies, his two best friends, Earl and Braxton. Earl, Braxton, Jayden, and I would hang out every weekend, similar to how I had with my old group of friends. There was one significant difference that enabled an increase in our deviant behaviors and marijuana consumption.

We had something any sophomore in high school would die for: our own apartment. It was not necessarily classified as an apartment by state regulations, but it was damn close. Mr. and Mrs. Powers owned a detached building built behind the main house. This building included a spacious apartment located above a four-car garage. The apartment was a three bedroom/one-bathroom apartment that we would stay at almost every weekend. The apartment was nearly 900 square feet. It was a fantasy for most teenagers, but reality for us.

This apartment had an attic, which we used so much we might as well have called it our second story. In addition, this apartment could be considered the igniter to my fire of addiction. The attic in particular was used for our deviant behaviors. We would smoke marijuana every weekend consistently there, and it was strategically planned. First of all, it was so soundproofed that you could not even hear the TV in the apartment blaring. This was important due to the fact that Jayden had dogs that would awake and bark if they detected any movement or noise on the premises. Secondly, the strong aroma could not pass the sealed attic entrance. Lastly, there was not a ladder to access the attic, therefore you had to climb into the attic. The reason why this plan was flawless was we knew that Jayden's parents were not capable of climbing into the attic even on the off chance they wanted to. If they needed something fixed or brought down from the attic it was Jayden and I who did it.

We had a flawless procedure, to the point that it was inevitable we'd get away with it. Jayden, Earl, and I were always blazing up, loving our state of hysteria. Notice I did not say Braxton; he knew that what we were doing was wrong. With that said, he refused to participate in these guilt-filled activities. He would stay downstairs, and rarely gave in to our subconscious peer pressure. Curiosity would occasionally get the best of him, though, so he would decide to experiment. It was always a delightful surprise when Braxton would smoke, because we saw it as him "living a little."

Braxton's experimentation ended quickly once his dearest friend Earl was caught after his father was building suspicion. Earl's father administered an at-home drug test that Earl inevitably failed due to the festivities that were taking place at Jayden's residence. Once the drug test came back positive for THC, his father was outraged. His father then raided his room like a police officer scavenging a murderer's apartment. His father ripped apart his dresser, looked through his bookbag, and even thoroughly searched inside all of his clothing. The intensive search concluded with Earl's father finding a small bag of marijuana, and he now knew the test was not a false positive like Earl attempted to claim it was. Following the search, Earl was interrogated; consequently, Jayden's name was thrown in the story.

The word got to Mr. and Mrs. Powers... Mrs. Powers stormed up the apartment stairs pondering three different scenarios: **1)** Earl is lying to save another (closer) friend, **2)** Earl's father simply has this all wrong, or **3)** I am dragging Jayden out of that apartment, and no one will ever be permitted in there again. She swung the door open, and searched the entire place like a maniac. She came up with absolutely nothing due to the fact that everything was stashed in the attic.

"Mom, I am being used as a scapegoat," Jayden pleaded.

I went along with the story. I did not want to lose the privilege of being at Jayden's, and we mutually dreaded the idea of our marijuana smoking decreasing. His parents believed us, because we were the two innocent best friends. Mrs. Powers could not fathom her precious boy ever doing something so wrong.

Let me make a point here: this is a blatant red flag that addiction is now spawning, and is not just habitual fun. I state that because we "threw Earl under the bus." For minor fun that is meaningless, you would not sacrifice a friendship; an addict who is falling in love with their poison of choice will, though. So even though marijuana is not chemically addictive, the action itself can be. This is a symptom of developing addiction that comes out very early, but is typically completely ignored.

Obviously, Earl drifted away. Braxton also started to drift away when our deceitful weekend nights would come around due to the sinful deception and lies that revolved around it. He was in a troublesome situation; his two best friends were going against all of his values and morals.

The reality of this situation would be:

We showed our demonic side throwing Earl under the bus. It was completely wrong to let Earl go down singlehandedly, and also to lie after being caught red-handed. The direct result of those devilish actions was Earl moving on with his life, which is exactly what he should have done. Braxton was not going to act in the same fashion as Jayden and I; he was living above the influence and lies, as he should have.

An addict's perception of the situation would be:

Earl is a moron, and got caught. That is not our problem… Earl is now just blaming us, because he does not want to blame himself for being caught. If he were a real friend, he would have kept our names out of it. Honestly, we do not need friends like him anyway. As far as Braxton goes, he just listens to what his mom says. Braxton is cool; he is just too much of a "goody-goody," and if he were a good friend, he would accept us for who we are.

They were not the only two that we deceived with our substance issues at such a young age. Jayden and I also had a good friend named Stephanie whom we deceived as well. She would have no part in drug using, so we could never tell her what Jayden and I were doing.

Stephanie was extremely involved with our local private Catholic school. Marijuana usage was absolutely unacceptable in the eyes of her primary network of friends. Even though Stephanie was not having a part in any sort of drug usage, her brother would happily rip the bong with us. Roger, Stephanie's brother, was younger than the rest of us by a couple years. Even though he was younger, he was "mature" for his age and typically hung out with the older crowd. The reality of the situation is he was deviating from his age group, therefore he attempted to enter a population where it was socially acceptable, making it less shameful.

It was Labor Day and Jayden's parents had the day off. So since they were home the entire day, we decided to go smoke with Stephanie's younger brother and a new member of the group named Steven, in the attic of Stephanie's residence above the garage. Stephanie would kill us if she witnessed us smoking, let alone with her little brother. Stephanie was supposed to be at practice till later on that day, but she was informed practice was cancelled due to rain as soon as she got there. As she was walking up her driveway, she heard our laughter coming from her attic in her detached garage. Wondering what was in the attic, she ran up the wooden ladder.

Once she heard it was us, she started pounding on the ceiling, screaming, "Let me in, I can smell what you're doing! Along with the entire neighborhood!"

At first, we sat in silence as if she would just go away. Filled with aggravation, she threatened to call her mother if we did not evacuate the attic. We stared at one another for a second.

Her brother sarcastically yelled, "Okay! We will be coming down momentarily."

Stephanie was outraged, and threatened to never speak to us again. Of course, we snaked our way out of her outrage by being extremely apologetic. We looked remorseful and promised we would quit smoking at that very moment, even though we had some more pot waiting for us at the house. Here is deceiving a friend once again.

Stephanie's perception would be something close to:

Jayden and Brad have pulled my last straw; they know I do not want them harming themselves. But they didn't just do that - they also engaged my brother at my own house! I cannot believe they would do such a thing!

Our perception was:

She is just like Braxton, just a conformer. Catholic school messed her up in the head… It is not like we got her brother into marijuana; he would have smoked it anyway. If anything, we made it a safer environment for him. We cannot be responsible for what he does, and plus it is not like we are making him do it. Another thing – just because Stephanie does not smoke does not mean we can't – this is horse crap!

Wow, talk about contradicting perceptions. Even though the bottom perception is completely wrong, it has a sense of legitimacy to it. Approximately 22.6 million Americans would find the bottom response a realistic explanation of the situation. (That is the number of drug users in America as of 2013.) The point of explaining this contribution to my addiction is to dig deeper in the complex and drawn-out process of becoming an addict. I do not believe if your kid is caught smoking marijuana that they must be sent to an intensive in-house rehabilitation. In fact, it would be counterintuitive, they will probably come out worse. The point I am trying to make is not necessarily that inhaling marijuana showed me that I was developing a substance abuse issue. The point here is that I was deceiving, lying, and doing whatever was necessary to continue my smoking habits. This started by hanging out with Marcus, and continually progressed with Jayden. I even sacrificed a good friend to continue my habit.

I had now metaphorically started dating my abuser(s). This was my first step on the dark road of addiction. At this point in time, I did not see the light of such a huge problem. My perception was that we'd found the three new amigos: Jayden, myself, and marijuana (without any chance of doing the "hard stuff"). What I am doing in the "perception" above is making excuses for my drug while outraging loved ones. These are all signs of a developing addict that I wish I had known way before hitting my rock bottom.

Once again, a pot smoker does not necessarily mean that the individual is an addict in the making. Honestly, in many scenarios this is not the case. On the other hand, once someone is defending their metaphoric "abuser" by lying, making justifications, and even deceiving close friends, they have a high risk of having addictive traits that they must learn to control. If this kind of individual does not grasp the reality of the situation, they will eventually plummet to rock bottom. It will be impossible to get away from addiction if you are following these patterns at a young age. The main point of this section is to comprehend the signs of the addictive personality. Cocaine, MDMA (aka Molly), heroin, or meth usage plays out identically to the situation(s) above. If you or someone you know replicates these actions directed toward friends and loved ones I recommend you or they get help immediately. There is a large difference between an addict and a habitual marijuana smoker, and with the knowledge in this chapter, I hope you see those differences. The occasional marijuana smoker will not risk friendships and persecution, or be so deceitful. On the other hand, a developing addict certainly will.

This is similar to many childhood experiences, and by no means is the end of my deviance. As I explained, I feel most stories about addiction (as well as overdosing) only have the tragedy. This is why people do not comprehend what an addict is, and how drawn out the process is. All the masses see is how the individual ingested their last dosage before death, prison, or recovery. I hope with this section people will grasp where addiction starts before it leads to scars, time in the system, rock bottom, and death.

III.
Justification and Comparison

"THE EXPLANATION"

THE DEFINITION OF COMPARISON:

A. To consider or describe as similar, equal, or analogous; liken.
B. To examine in order to note the similarities or differences of.

So how does comparing give us false perceptions, and, even more so, enable us to take actions such as using drugs on a daily basis? Like I stated several times, the road to addiction is a complex process. Comparing can deepen addiction subconsciously, and is one of the most detrimental aspects to addiction. It is a tool of justification that can give a sense of innocence to your sinful doings. Comparison, justification, and falsified innocence work simultaneously to enhance addiction. It is an aspect of addiction that recovery programs often overlook, and it becomes so natural that we are unaware we are doing it. This is extremely bothersome to me because I feel it is the biggest contributor to deepening addiction and it is completely ignored. I do not think it is ignored on purpose, but ignorance is bliss. Comparing is something humans have the ability to do, and whether for good or evil, we use this humanistic mind tool every day.

For example, how do you know how pretty, skinny, cool, or rich you are? It is all comparing. If you are annually making 25,000 U.S.D., then you can assume you are not rich. In fact, depending on inflation rates and the cost of living in particular cities, you could be considered poverty stricken. Now, bring that to Ethiopia, and you will be worshiped like royalty. These are opposite connotations, one being poverty and the other wealth. Everything depends on your perception, and your perception often blossoms from comparison. So you may ask how this relates to drugs, and that answer is simple. You can easily compare yourself to another addict on a different substance, using at a different age, or to an individual who uses the substance more often. You can compare to anything or anyone to make yourself feel better about the actions that you partake in.

For example, you often here drinkers compare themselves to marijuana smokers. You will hear drinkers say such things as "At least what I am doing is legal, and I am not ruining my brain." On the other hand, the marijuana smoker can say, "At least I am not getting violent, getting convicted of DUIs, and unable to walk straight." That is fine and dandy, and makes you feel what you are doing is acceptable. This is why addicts utilize their ability to compare. It is acceptable to an addict, because they are comparing themselves to other individuals who may be on a darker path than them. An alcohol consumer will not compare himself to the president of America or his pastor. This comparison will make him look bad in his own self-perception. It will not help the human's "self-fulfilling prophecy" they are looking for. It is human nature to think more highly of yourself while simultaneously worsening your perception of other individuals. The self-fulfilling prophecy of finding innocence through comparison is in continual action when it comes to an addict's mindset.

This is causing a deception of self-reflection. When you are looking in the mirror you are seeing a different person than your loved ones are seeing. You see a normal human being that just seeks a free-spirited good time, although your loved ones are seeing the complete opposite. Your loved ones grasp and internalize the reality of the monster being made. You have this false perception because you are justifying your drug.

Keep in mind that perception is your reality, and your reality is "I am doing fine." You truly believe that you are on the right road even if you are using substances. Well, how is this perception being seen as a reality even possible? Our perception is our reality, but how can anyone truly interpret a promising future on drugs? You believe you are on the right path, because the guy over there is doing harder drugs or doing the drug more often. You compare yourself to others who will make you seem to be doing okay. The addict will compare using anything that is applicable, including, but not limited to: age, duration of usage, reasons for usages, current troubles, localities, and even something as ridiculous as gender.

You will often hear younger individuals developing their addiction say, "Well, I am only fifteen and he is twenty-four and still doing drugs. I know I will quit WAY before that." They are using age as a factor for justification. A fifteen-year-old does not see many twenty-four-year olds doing drugs, therefore making it unacceptable by society for the elder to do so. The fifteen-year-old is making it seem more acceptable to do the drug by comparing a more troubled addict using age as the primary factor. This is nonsense, especially since the fifteen-year-old can essentially become that twenty-four-year-old in nine years. If the fifteen-year-old continues to think in this fashion, they WILL be that twenty-four-year-old before they know it.

Some people will say, "I am only doing this drug because I want to, not because I need to." This is extremely common in addicts. This may be the most common justification amongst drug users. Individuals do not want to admit they NEED something, and an easy solution is to simply say you "want" the substance for enjoyment. It makes you feel as if you are in control; regardless of whether you are or aren't, it will ease the consciousness. To distinguish whether you are "wanting" it or "needing" it is extremely difficult. With that said, this comparison of "wanting vs. needing" consists of a lot of ambiguity, making it an easy comparison to form a falsified reality.

For example, person A may be using drugs at a party, but person B uses them when he/she is stressed out and home alone. Well, person A read in a recovery book that an addict is defined based on why they use a substance, therefore they are not an addict – they just do it for fun. This is fine, and to be honest it is factual. My question is, if person A encounters the same troubles and hardship person B does, will they turn to the substance?

Here is an example to further explain how ambiguous this comparison can be. It is possible that when a tragedy does happen person A wants to go to a party to keep their mind off things. At that party, person A sedates him/herself with their poison of choice. So that's fine, person A is doing it at a party because they want to; they're not like person B, who feels they need it in their studio apartment all alone. It is simply just for fun on the grounds that person A is at a party and it is offered to him. The next day, person A is still in depression from the tragedy. Person A goes to their buddy's house to once again get their mind off of how life has been treating them. They decide to use their substance again, and once again claim, "Because I want it, I do not need it." Are they doing this with friends as pure occasional enjoyment or masking the reality that they are becoming addicted to a substance?

You keep telling yourself that you only "want" it. Many addicts claim this, because the hardest thing to say is "I am an addict." Those four words seem to strip you of your independence, and have a connotation of failure, worthlessness, and hopelessness due to the stigma our country has given to the addict. The fact of the matter is, you know that you will feel like a failure, like you have nothing, and feel hopelessness if you come to the conclusion that you are an addict. This is the reason so many addicts can't, or will not, say those four words.

Sure, those four words suck, but there is a bright side to them. The benefit of stating "I am an addict" is that it creates a moment where you have the opportunity to ricochet from your rock bottom. This is where you can rebuild and start your journey to recovery. This is a hard point of view to grasp, so newly developing addicts would much rather say, "I want it, I do not need it." With that said, they falsify reality by comparing themselves to addicts who need it, when they "truly just want it."

So what does comparing do? It justifies the wrongdoings. According to Teal Swan, "If you're trying to justify something, you're trying to escape from something that you don't want to admit to." In my opinion, the most dangerous characteristic of an addict regarding the probability of the addiction becoming more severe is comparison and justification. The more you use comparison accompanied by justification, the deeper your addiction will become. This is all typically subconscious, because you are developing a false perception that you perceive as reality. The point of this section is to obtain a more thorough understanding of addiction. It starts with your loss of innocence, but this is how it deepens. All you need is the deadly duo of comparison and justification.

"ORDERING A DEEP-END ADDICTION WITH A SIDE OF COMPARISON"

JAYDEN AND I WOULD BE FORTUNATE to say that Stephanie was the last person we outraged with our deceitful ways. Our addiction started to deepen, although there was a plateau timeframe. What I mean by a plateau timeframe is the duration your addiction is stagnant. For example, it could be defined as the era of only smoking marijuana (the so-called "gateway drug"), or the timeframe an alcoholic only drinks at night. Many addicts were at a point in their life when they only smoked marijuana or drank at times that society deems acceptable (e.g. Friday after work). Addicts start with a minimally addictive drug, using at minimal occurrences, and then gradually progress from there. I used the term "plateau timeframe" to describe the era in addiction where you would not even fathom doing a harder drug (or searching for the "next high"). The plateau timeframe is the best opportunity to get through to an addict, but how does the plateau timeframe spiral into an increase in consuming drugs?

As with most hardships in life, it will not happen overnight. With that said, this section is to explain how my addictive personality spiraled out of control. This chapter will explain how my addiction deepened, leading me to my rock bottom. Like I said in the second section, at this point in time my drug usage was simply using marijuana as a habitual weekend getaway. School, lacrosse, and studying filled the weekdays, not smoking cannabis. This chapter will demonstrate how that changed subconsciously in the natural phenomenon of drug addiction.

This era of addiction blossomed from Jayden impressing his parents through his athletic and scholarly achievements. He was applying for colleges, and demonstrating he truly had a bright future. To compensate for Jayden's achievements, his parents allowed him to stay in the detached apartment full time, rather than just the weekend nights. They had no idea they were making a terrible decision. Keep in mind that we convinced his parents that we had no part in Earl's marijuana usage. In fact, in their eyes we were sober birds. We were young adults who had always been law-abiding citizens. In the eyes of Mr. and Mrs. Powers, we were the two innocent best friends who mutually benefited one another.

Jayden brought all of his belongings up to the detached apartment. There were couches in the living room, beds in the bedrooms, a stereo system, and a fifty-inch plasma TV in the living room. His new residence came together as something that a high-school student could only wish for. When we had gotten him all moved in, we decided that we needed to furnish the "second story," the attic. Instead of a bed we had ashtrays, instead of a stereo we had posters, instead of a TV we had lighters, and instead of couches we had paraphernalia. This completed the "second story" of our new place, and would be any high-school kid's road to addiction. It was a VIP smoke spot that was even known around our local high-school peers not affiliated with our direct network of friends.

Everything was great for Jayden, but for me it stayed as stagnant as before. Keep in mind that I would reside in the apartment every weekend, therefore the only difference for me was the newly added furniture. I was partially jealous that Jayden had the benefit of staying there every night. This fact made me realize that he could smoke every night, making it a daily getaway rather than a weekly occasion. Every Friday night, I would be the happiest person in the world, anxious to spend the weekend with my best friend, blazing up. I was so excited for the weekend ahead that I could not describe it in words. On the other hand, I would start to dread Sunday night starting the same Sunday morning, because I knew I would have to leave my fantasy lifestyle and enter back into the reality of rules and structure. I wanted to figure out a way to stay over there more often, essentially to lie to my father to stay out on school nights.

This is another example of an addict in the making;
I am lying once again to the man that loves me the most for my drug.

I contemplated on a lie to tell my father. I felt bad about it at the beginning – essentially, this was the point where I was losing my innocence even further. After contemplating for days on end, I finally found what I could intertwine with Jayden to make my father allow me to sleep there: studying. This lie not only would grant me permission to stay at Jayden's but also make my father proud. I figured I could just tell him that Jayden and I had made a pact for straight As, therefore I would be over at Jayden's several nights a week focusing on our "academics."

This was a flawless lie, and made my father confident that I was making good decisions as a young man. Consequently, I was persistently staying at Jayden's nearly three or four times a week. This directly resulted in the two of us turning into chronic marijuana smokers. You could bet your bottom dollar we would smoke every night I stayed there. We would wake up and go to school together after a long night of inhaling cannabis smoke. This was difficult at first, but with time it became habitual and routinized.

This started to affect me physically, and although my father was naïve my mother knew exactly what was going on. My mother lived 3,000 miles away. My mother lived in Los Angeles, which was clear across the country from our small Virginia town. My mother could tell in my voice and attitude that I was experimenting with marijuana. This might have been because my mother lived the same party lifestyle I'd started to merge into, unlike my father, who lived above the influence.

My mother was not the only loved one who caught on to my addiction. My father's wife also was assuming devilish activities were going on at Jayden's house, and she made that clear in her attitude toward me. My stepmother and I never got along well, but people did not faze me at this point in life. I never really was affected by what people thought, or even how they acted toward me. This is pretty common with addicts consumed by drugs and their addictive personalities. This was not the primary reason I did not care for my stepmother. Her outlook on several aspects of life was flawed, but she sure was right about me smoking marijuana.

Regardless of how I felt, I knew this was an opportunity for me to stay at Jayden's full time; essentially, I thought, "full-time smoking!" I thought this could potentially mean my best friend and I could smoke every night of the week in our private VIP addict den. I decided I was going to propose staying at Jayden's full time due to the fact that my stepmother and I didn't get along. I figured I would tell my father that this was an opportunity to relieve everyone of stress. I promised him I would still come home to see him every day. After days of consideration he agreed, and at age sixteen I was living on my own with no parental supervision.

As time went on, I was staying at Jayden's five to six times a week, which eventually turned into the entire week. In no time, I moved all my belongings into Jayden's apartment, and our friends now saw it as "our" apartment. I literally had nothing left at my father's residence. The only thing that I used the house for was documentation for legality purposes. Even though I had developed an array of benefits to staying at Jayden's, there was one that was prominent and most important – it was awesome knowing that no matter what obstacles I encountered during the day, marijuana was there to make it better.

Bingo! This is where I can look back and depict exactly where my addiction was brewing to a deeper level. This is potentially the biggest sign of addiction. I am now dependent on my drug for relieving my daily stressors. I had moved out at sixteen with the primary reasoning of unlimited marijuana consumption and minimal supervision. My body had not necessarily developed a chemical addiction, but my psyche had now started a process of becoming dependent on a high to relieve my typical and daily stressors. Even though there is no chemical addiction in this situation, the danger stems from potentially developing the mindset of chasing the "next high."

Jayden and I hit a plateau era for a relatively long time. Once again, I mean being satisfied with the simplistic marijuana high. Marijuana releases dopamine to put you in a relaxed state and mindset to alter your views on certain stressors. People will say it is potent, and it is even classified as a mild hallucinogen. If you have inhaled marijuana you would say this statement is exaggerated, and would probably conclude it just made you laugh, hungry, and then tired. This is typically the routine, and we were satisfied with that. Many kids our age were smoking, and to be honest it became so common it had the "innocent" connotation to our population. It was similar to sneaking out – it might not be completely innocent, but by all means was socially accepted by the high-school population.

The issue of addiction is not necessarily started by marijuana, but what happens when the marijuana high no longer makes the cut? What happens when it is no longer being high, but rather a new sober? I say new sober because most drug addicts started smoking occasionally, which was identical to my situation. When this feeling becomes addictive, you want to feel that feeling more often. Notice I said the feeling of being "high" is addictive, not the drug itself.

Logically, if something is bringing happiness to your life you want more. This mindset is mutually shared by a plethora of people, but the dilemma for addicts is this: regardless of the harm it causes you, it is impossible for you to say no. An addict has no sense of moderation. An addict has the mindset of "the more the merrier" as long as it brings happiness, even though the joy is only short-term. To complement this mindset, you smoke more often, possibly smoking every night. From there, you want this feeling more often than every night; consequently, you smoke throughout the day. Essentially, you are making the marijuana "stoned" the new sober. At such a young age I was consuming such an enormous amount that I considered myself "sober" while under the influence of marijuana, and simply miserable without it.

We started smoking on the go with various people in their vehicle(s). We would smoke before school, during lunch, after school, and then in the attic before bed. Smoking every two to four hours now forced us to go about daily functioning while high. When you are a chronic smoker it becomes so natural it is a sober for you. It is similar to how people use nicotine, which people tend to forget is merely just another drug. You smoke a cigarette for the first time and become buzzed. After smoking for a long period of time you develop the habit of using nicotine throughout the day, removing the associated buzz.

Once you have reached this point, it is just so natural that the body needs it, and it is so routinized into your lifestyle that you function perfectly fine after inhaling a cigarette. This is an identical cycle to the chronic smoker's. I was smoking marijuana on a consistent basis all day every day, but I was maintaining and balancing honor-roll academics, working at a local grocery store, and playing lacrosse. All of this was done with dopamine receptors acting rapidly, and I became so used to it no one even knew I was smoking before any of these duties. I was living life as an individual would sober. So if marijuana causes no harm, you can eventually function while stoned, and even public figures have admitted to smoking weed, why is it so harmful?

Well, you now can classify marijuana as my gateway drug. It was my key to unlock a real addiction. From this point, it is highly probable an addict will chase the next high. The strength and consistency of the next drug and its usage can fluctuate depending on the individual, but regardless, most drugs besides marijuana will now offer the chemical dependency to accompany the already developed mental addiction to being high. Whether the new poison of choice is cocaine, an opiate, a methamphetamine, an amphetamine, a barbiturate, or any other drug or derivative of those listed, you will start to develop a chemical dependency. Once again, the rate of becoming a full-blown addict fluctuates from person to person, but it is only a matter of time before it happens if the addiction is not contained.

When I say the "new" drug, I do not simply mean trading marijuana for a narcotic. It is not as simple as trading one for another. Typically, addicts will hold their old drug while simultaneously starting to use the new one. You use the "old" drug primarily with a miniscule addition of the "new" drug. It is similar to changing your pet's food. When changing your furry friend's daily diet, you are supposed to gradually transfer the new food into the old food. Drugs share the same philosophy. An addict uses the "new," or next, drug, until they are habitually using one or both of them. This is where people mistake the word "gateway." Addicts will continue with chronic marijuana smoking, or the "old" drug, while doing the new drug occasionally. You have now entered a cycle. Refer back to my description of the progression of marijuana use: occasional, habitual, daily, and then chronic. Addicts will typically enter an identical cycle with their new drug, and that is the exact cycle Jayden and I entered.

"What's up, Jayden, ever tried ecstasy?" asked a peer of Jayden's.

"Well, no, never even seen it," Jayden responded.

This was similar to the other deviance examples I used in the previous section – at first there was no interest. He walked out of his third block class not being intrigued by the question at all, although the lack of interest would not last. Later on in the week, the classmate had brought some with him and Jayden was asked again, and curiosity started kicking in. He was intrigued by the peer's description of the drug. It seemed it was a more of an intense high than the marijuana, especially because being stoned became less and less potent. Jayden's friend described it as seeing vibrant colors, mildly hallucinating, and being in a state of euphoria.

Being frequently stoned and unsatisfied, Jayden and I had been contemplating trying this drug, but promised ourselves we would only try it once to see what a "real high" was like. We resisted for quite some time until we talked to Jayden's neighbor, Christian. Christian had a best friend whom I have ironically already introduced – Marcus. Marcus and Christian were into drugs long before we were, and they became a mentor for our usage of drugs. While Jayden and I were attempting to keep our heads straight with lacrosse they were experimenting further with drugs, a road that Jayden and I would soon replicate. They convinced us that ecstasy was not necessarily a bad drug.

Our biggest issue that instilled fear was the possibility that it would be "cut" with other drugs, such as cocaine. We had always heard of cocaine being horrible, but had never heard much about ecstasy. Our "mentors" convinced us it did not mean anything, because they were as naïve as we were. Keep in mind how I stressed the importance of geological factors in addiction. All the "bad" kids in our beautiful Virginia town seem to be the upper-class cocaine users, and ecstasy was found in the neighboring district several miles south. With that said, there was not too much criticism regarding ecstasy, simply because not many people in our high school heard of the negative impact it has. In our perception, this meant there were no negative impacts besides the fact that it was a drug. The fact of the matter is, regardless of what the truth might have been, it made us feel a whole lot better about our desire for experimentation.

That Friday night rolled around, and we decided to execute what we had been desiring for the last week. We were very nervous, and we took major precautions to avoid doing something crazy. We obviously knew it was wrong if we were taking precautions. You take precautions because there is a realistic chance something can go wrong, therefore we consciously knew what we were doing was not the right action to be taking. This can also go back to innocence. We were losing more innocence with this new step into the drug world.

Is this where there is no applicable "innocence"? The answer to that is dictated by whether or not the particular population, network, etc. finds it socially acceptable.

Keep in mind the philosophical approach to innocence: it is as complex as addiction itself. I am implying another transition out of innocence here due to the fact that we consciously knew we were committing a devilish act, hence the precautions. The precautions were necessary, because deep down we knew this was a bad idea. Regardless of the instilled fear, we decided to follow through with it.

Another sign of an addict. I felt as if I were in the same situation when I took my first hit of marijuana. I was so nervous my hands were shaking, so confused I could not ease my mind, and so anxious that I just wanted to pop the damn pill… These pills were like ones I have never encountered in my life. It was a vibrant yellow with a vivid peace sign carved in the center of the pill, and the pill was obviously not manufactured by a pharmaceutical company. As nervous as I was, I still popped the pill without hesitation.

The chair was jammed underneath the golden doorknob of Jayden's apartment to ensure that, if we were too influenced under the drug, it would be more difficult to leave the premises. We also had a "sober monitor" named Steven. Steven had just started hanging out at the apartment, and was nonjudgmental of our decision to take the pills, although he wanted no part of it.

If you recall, Steven was at Stephanie's apartment the day she caught us smoking with her little brother. He still smoked marijuana, but had the same mindset Jayden and I had had a month prior – "All I will ever do is smoke marijuana." Steven smoked while Jayden and I were waiting for the ecstasy to kick in. We waited for fifteen minutes, and were unsure if we'd gotten ripped off. We were not used to a waiting period. This was due to the fact that marijuana hits you momentarily, if not instantly. As soon as we started to lose hope, the TV became much brighter. My face blossomed into the biggest smile I have ever had. The smile extended ear to ear. I was the happiest I have ever been in my entire life, although we were doing absolutely nothing.

Euphoria is something I never felt in its truest form till that night. I was feeling my body, and it felt as if they were someone else's hands. I doted upon my clothes, blankets, and other materials. Every material felt orgasmic to my skin. When I went to the bathroom my pupils were enormous and looked as if they were a close up of an insect's eye. I now understood why people said your pupils are "bugged out" on drugs. This feeling was amazing, and I felt stupid for fearing it in the first place. Hours later I realized the high was still there. That was remarkable, because I had been used to sixty-minute highs from the marijuana. This drug was out of this world, and amplified the affects that marijuana has on the brain.

Refer back to what I said regarding the new and old poisons of choice. The new drug does not necessarily replace the old one; instead it augments the old one. This is exactly how the night took place. In the next chapter of our night we found ourselves in the attic smoking, which enhanced the high even more. Once we left the attic, it was nearly 4:00 a.m. The ecstasy somehow gave us this willpower to stay up the entire night. We had no appetite, thirst, or desire to sleep. From 4:00 a.m. to roughly 6:00 a.m., we were crashing hard. We went from being full of life to lifeless during the earlier hours of the morning. Steven had been out for hours while Jayden and I were wide awake, but around 6:15 a.m., we joined him in an unconscious state of mind.

"Dude, it is two o'clock in the afternoon, guys!" Steven yelled.

I lifted my head up as if it had been nailed by a Mack truck the previous night. It took a significant amount of effort to lift my body off the couch, and it took another ten minutes before I could understand what Steven was saying.

Jayden woke up on the couch next to mine simultaneously. "Why the hell did you wake me up?" Jayden moaned, having no idea of the time.

"Well, I have been up since 11:00 a.m.! You guys have been motionless for hours, I was worried you were dying," explained Steven in a comical tone of voice.

It went from the best night of my life to the worst morning I have ever encountered. Jayden and I felt very grimy and dirty, not to mention extremely dehydrated. I had never felt so gross, self-conscious, and disgusted with my life. I felt that I had committed murder by taking a harder drug, and essentially did something I'd promised myself I would never do. The day after was terrible, and it was like I could not feel any type of happiness. After reminiscing for hours about the previous night, Jayden and I swore we would never let either of us do that again. We were convinced it was a one-time thing to fulfill our curiosity.

We felt so bad that we'd started to deepen our addiction, but with that simple action of comparing we could easily relieve the burden. This is where we now compared our lives to others in a worse situation. Metaphorically, we committed a crime, so let's find someone who has committed more crimes to give us a vision of ourselves as innocent. Comparing can form an internal innocence when you know society would not justify your wrong doings. Once again, this tool of comparison is extremely detrimental in deepening an addiction due to the fact that it makes you feel innocent and content with your self-image. It makes you believe that even though you are doing drugs, you at are not doing them as much or as often as the individual you are comparing yourself to. This evil action of comparing is something Jayden and I started doing, and it was making us feel better about the face in the mirror we encountered every time we decided to deepen our addiction.

We only did it once, so us saying we were not ecstasy users was a pretty rational excuse, right? Well, what happens when the ecstasy rolls around again? This would be the true test. It is easy to refuse something when it is not there. This why people will be clean in prison or a rehabilitation clinic, but then get back together with their poison of choice once they are back in society. The idea of ecstasy didn't appear in my thoughts for a couple weeks; instead I thought of the dreadful hangover that accompanied it. As soon as I thought the idea of doing any harder drugs was diminished, Marcus and Christian asked us how our experience was. This inevitably made us ponder the night again. We let them know without hesitation that the next morning was so terrible it was not even worth the fantastic night we'd had before it. We continued by explaining how the morning after consisted of a pounding headache and haziness, and that made us never want to try it again.

"Did you drink orange juice?" Christian asked.

Drinking orange juice had never come to mind. We had no need for a thirst quencher, or any appetite. He then went on to explain how the active chemicals in ecstasy will dehydrate the body, and that is why we felt so bad afterward. With that said, he concluded we should try the drug again the "right" way. Once again, this peer pressure is not on purpose; it is spawned from the situation. If we never would have tried the ecstasy this conversation would have never happened, but unfortunately for us it did happen and the temptation was very real.

The pathetic reality was we wanted to try it with the orange juice and get the full effect. This was just an asinine excuse to do the drug again, and we were deceiving ourselves to consume the drug the "right way." We were using something as miniscule as orange juice to ingest the drug again. The issue was that Jayden and I had said we would not let the other do it again; we made a pact to stay away from it. This initiated a lot of contemplating, and of course justifying the contemplation. We both deeply wanted to say let's try it again, but by the same token neither of us wanted to be the guy who said screw it – let's do it. After a lot of discussions back and forth on the subject we decided we would just determine our final decision when Jayden's friend offered it again.

In about a week Jayden's guy told him he had some "Yin Yangs" coming soon. Even though Jayden did not really know the difference, he acted like he did. He told his friend that he would let him know if he could get the money. Money was not an issue due to the fact that we were selling marijuana at the time. This made it possible to have "free" money. This money was all disposable income that we would typically spend on paraphernalia or other items that we definitely had no business buying. The reasoning behind the delayed answer was that he wanted to ask me what we should do. After school that day he told me about the situation, and I finally said screw it, let's get them.

"Okay, but it's seriously the last time – okay!?" Jayden asked with a serious look.

"Of course, man," I responded. "We might as well experience the drug the right way."

We were going fifty-five miles per hour, anxiously waiting for what the guy called "Yin Yangs." While we were sitting in the car, the guy hopped in the backseat, startling the both of us.

His eyes were about to pop out of his head and his breath smelled like marijuana and booze. "This will get ya real nice bruh, yeah bruh, real niceee…"

We had never seen someone act or talk in such a slurred and murmured dialog. He seemed like he was under the influence, only like they showed on *COPS* or MTV, and that caught Jayden and me by surprise. I was partially scared, but also partially excited. This addict in me was really starting to hit the surface, and I seemed to start chasing the next high. Even though this worried me, I knew Jayden would never let me go down the wrong path. I knew deep down Jayden would not let me slip into my guilty desires.

We pulled up in Jayden's driveway. He was very nervous, and I was more on the excited side. We called Steven over again, but Steven was busy with academics. We still decided to continue with our adventurous night. We again were in a place we'd promised ourselves we wouldn't be in, doing a harder drug once again. We did this by throwing a little justification in there, which was that we needed to experience the real thing. The "real" effect would blossom from the idiotic excuse to accompany the drug with orange juice. Very ignorant and irrational to think, but regardless we sat back and waited for Jayden's parents to fall asleep so we could pop these "Yin Yangs," and experience our euphoria once again.

"Goodnight, Jayden," Mrs. Powers said over the telephone. Jayden concluded the phone call in his bedroom in the detached apartment. He hung up the phone, and walked out of his room where he saw me watching *Two and Half Men*. "Well, my mom is going to bed," said Jayden. "So let's just give it about thirty more minutes to be safe."

This is the only precaution we took. This time we did not have a sober monitor, the chair locking the door, or any other worries in the world because all we cared about was the fact that we were going to be euphoric in a couple short hours. This is another characteristic of addiction I will explain at a later point in time: carelessness. Essentially we did not care about anything (e.g. getting caught), because we knew we were with our poison of choice. It had been about three weeks since we tried our first ecstasy pill, and we were ready for the second.

We popped the pills simultaneously, fully prepared with the two personal bottles of Orange Juice. We were ready to now experience the ecstasy high the "right way." These "Yin Yangs" had a different look than the last ones, but the feelings were identical. The only difference was these pills made my tongue numb, so I decided to call Christian. He informed us that this pill was cut with more cocaine, which made me feel like a miserable piece of scum. Once again, this was because my area saw cocaine as much worse than ecstasy, although the reality is they are equally as harmful, dangerous, and addictive. These facts made me feel terrible about myself, but as soon as the effects kicked in I could not care less about the harm it was causing.

I was so happy; words do not exist to explain it. I was sweating an awful lot, so I would drink the Sunny D regularly. The blankets felt amazing brushing against my body, my skin felt smooth, I started to vibe to a genre I could not stand sober, and the orange juice felt so good. I felt each piece of pulp sliding down my throat. This feeling was more amazing than the first. I had no worries about school, relationships, work, lacrosse, or even my life as a whole. The night was mind-blowing until we took a hard crash around 6:00 a.m. Jayden passed out first with a gigantic smile on his face, and my eyes started to close falling asleep in a similar fashion.

That night was amazing, and to be honest the morning was not bad. I guess the orange juice really did work. Jayden and I decided that was the last time doing it, but it would only be a matter of time before another excuse would enter our minds. We felt bad, though, and as if our life was plummeting in a direction we did not want it to. This is a difficult reality to face. With that said, we decided not to. All we had to do was compare ourselves to someone walking on the same path to ease the guilt, and from there we felt justified for the deceitful acts. The comparing game we started to participate in became more irrational and dangerous every time.

We continued to compare ourselves to Christian and Marcus, and we would attempt to use the tool of comparing by saying absurd things. One comparison we used was the length of time using the drug. Christian and Marcus were using it for a much longer duration than we were. The reality is a drug consumer is a drug consumer, although this information will make someone feel better about themselves regarding the substance abuse that they are consumed by. We would also compare our educational plans. Jayden and I were college bound. Marcus wanted to just simply work after graduation, and Christian wanted to go to HVAC trade school. This is factual information as well, and shows the ambition we had may have been much greater than our two peers', but regardless was irrelevant to drug usage. A college-bound kid can easily drop at any given time. This can all be a direct result from using drugs. The comparison did not tarnish there. You can assume that your rate of comparison essentially correlates with the guilt you have within.

We would also compare how often we were doing the drug. Jayden and I would tell ourselves – we cannot be addicts; we only do this stuff occasionally. Christian and Marcus did drugs on a regular basis, even school nights. We did not take into consideration that we'd started smoking marijuana on the weekend, and as time went on had started using it habitually. Jayden and I never saw the identical trend that was happening.

Like I said, it is a cycle, and I call it a repeating cycle for a reason. We also did not ponder why we were doing it occasionally rather than as frequently as Christian and Marcus. There were several aspects to take into consideration, such as supply, time, and risk. First of all, we did not always have the ecstasy readily available, only on occasion. Secondly, Jayden's parents' supervision only allowed us to do it at night, and we were also dedicated to lacrosse. Marcus and Christian both knew more dealers than we did, Christian also had parents who were not strict in the slightest, and they both no longer played lacrosse.

We would even attempt our participation in lacrosse as an excuse. We would justify our actions by saying we had our priorities straight while those guys didn't. Well, though it was great that we were participating in school functions, it also had no relevance to drugs, but if you want to justify yourself you will find a way to intertwine the two.

The funny thing about drugs is your drive and ambition will inevitably tarnish while on them, but you try not to think about that. You may still be ambitious on drugs, but the drive will not be optimized. An addict's comparison and justification is similar to a buffet. They will only put what seems good on the "comparison/justification" plate, and they will disregard whatever does not look good. This is furthering that false reality that is developing. An addict's viewpoint can be described as "out of sight, out of mind," so if they see they are young, experimenting, and college bound this is their reality. The reality may be that they are a young and developing addict that soon will be another college dropout, but they keep that out of mind. Justification and comparison can be extremely dangerous, and it will continue to be used until you can snap out of lying to yourself and grasp reality.

The justification continued; we were constantly comparing ourselves to other addicts. Our psyche seemed to be deceiving us more and more as we were "experimenting" with the ecstasy. The ecstasy was fun, and it never turned into a daily activity, unlike the marijuana smoking. What the ecstasy did do was open the door of curiosity even wider. Ecstasy was the peephole to my addiction, and after I liked what I saw in the small peephole, I fell down the bottomless pit that was behind it.

As the door swung wide open, so did options of other drugs. Senior year of high school we started hearing of hallucinogens, uppers, and painkillers. Hallucinogens kind of instilled fear in Jayden and I, and uppers Jayden was prescribed. Jayden was prescribed an ADD medication by the name of Vyvanse. Since we did drugs together, I was not going to buy an upper similar to what Jayden was already prescribed. This left us with one option to explore, the painkiller. We figured it could not be that bad. I mean, honestly, I had been prescribed a painkiller for a broken arm, so I used that to justify my doings. "The government prescribed the drug, it could not be that bad." I figured if the government prescribes it then it cannot be that dangerous or addictive, and I obviously had a false perception. This is a huge misconception that is commonly accepted by the youth – "The drugs that the government prescribes are safer and less addictive." Regardless of the misconception, the painkiller was the next drug that consumed Jayden's and my curiosity. I am sure you can guess where Jayden and I got the painkillers – Marcus and Christian. They had a new addition to their circle named Logan. Logan was a year younger, but a lot more known in the drug world. Logan eventually became close with Jayden and I, and he would bring over Vicodin that was already crushed.

Keep in mind what I said about the old addiction and new addiction(s) intertwining with one another to develop a poly-substance abuse issue.

With that said, we would use the crushed Vicodin Logan brought over and put it on our marijuana blunts. This feeling was much different than the ecstatic ecstasy high. This high was a super "chill" high. The high that absorbed you into the couch. I never was on such a substance that made you happily be a couch potato. It was definitely different, but nonetheless amazing. My mind seemed as if it were on autopilot, which also gave me a careless mindset. With that said, I believe that is the high I was chasing since day one – pure carelessness. Shoulders were at ease and I had no problems running through my mind. After about two hours, I fell into a nice, deep, deathlike sleep. Jayden and I figured that this was something we could do on a weekday, because it does not keep you up that late. We did just that for a while. We would smoke with the prescription medication crushed and sprinkled over the green crystalized marijuana. We continued to break the pact to only be marijuana consumers, but to rationalize that fact we only needed a little more comparison and justification.

Well, at least we smoked it on a blunt! At least we were not snorting them like other people. If you are an addict reading this, I am sure that makes perfect sense to you. If you are not, I am sure this is as asinine as most people would see it. An addict that is subconsciously defending their "abuser" would think this is rational and completely logical. Similar to the metaphor in the beginning of the novel – "Yeah, he hit me, but at least it did not leave a mark." Well, the reality is he hit you, and the reality of this was we were consuming the pill. We even started to compare things that had not even happened yet, such as "quitting." We "knew" that when we turn eighteen, we would leave this life behind. We always thought of ourselves as better than other drug users, because we knew we were going to quit when we were legal adults.

Vicodin became more prevalent as the weeks of getting to know Logan went by. We continued to consume the chemicals through smoking them on a laced blunt of marijuana. We stayed stagnant in regards to the method of usage until one Friday night. We decided to snort them. I viciously sniffed the white powder as if it were my last breath of air I could take. Another terrible life event took place at that moment: I loved snorting the pill. The burning sensation brought fulfillment in the process of altering my state of mind. I do not know what it was; maybe I enjoyed feeling the pain. Maybe it was the fact that I was "paying the price" to get high. It almost gave me a physical representation of how much my mind was altering.

Let us go back to when Christian was a habitual marijuana smoker, and compare that to how we were now. We used to think that if you smoked marijuana on the weekdays you were going nowhere. So let's say we compared ourselves months prior to Christian and Marcus during the same timeframe. We would conclude that Christian smokes marijuana every day, and we only smoke it once a week. Christian quit lacrosse, and we didn't. The list of comparison can be infinite... Now let's use Christian's habitual smoking back in the day, and compare it to us in the present. Christian smokes marijuana every day, and he does nothing else. We thought that was terrible, but now we smoke marijuana every day as well as take Vicodin, and even ecstasy every once in a while. My point here is we are now worse than what we compared ourselves to originally. Keep in mind the buffet analogy.... we would never put that on our plate, it simply does not seem appealing for our comparison/justification plate.

Comparing is such a fluctuant and deceiving game that when a couple short months had passed Christian could compare himself to us, with us making him feel better about himself. Jayden and I brought three more drugs into our lives while Christian started and stuck with his painkillers. Those drugs we started to habitually use were Jayden's prescribed Vyvanse, Valium that we wrongfully obtained for free, and alcohol that we started consuming in copious amounts. These three all developed together.

Jayden started hanging around his older brother's friends who drank, and man did they drink. They were all military that fit the Ridge Run stereotype: drinking Bud Light at a bonfire, talking about females and hunting. They would let us drink with them on one condition: we were not doing anything else regarding drugs. They were attempting to give us the adventurous teen years we were dying for, and keep us safe in the process. It is similar to how parents will let an underage minor drink if it is in the safety of their home. Jayden's older family friends knew we were going to get intoxicated regardless of what they said. Therefore, they figured they would contribute in making it safe for us to drink without being dangerously unsupervised. Well, we started to love being drunk with them, but God knows we did not want to give up the other substances. What could we do?

Lie! We lied to and deceived all of Jayden's brother's friends. The older crowd figured they were saving us from not doing the drugs swarming the area, and boy were they wrong. Jayden's brother was traveling the world for our country as a member of the U.S. Infantry. As an Army man, he did not have much contact with his friends, and it was as if Jayden filled a missing part of his brother's friends' hearts. With that said, they loved to drink with us as much as we enjoyed drinking with them. Drinking became a routine such as marijuana, but started as something occasional. We started drinking on the weekends, in the same fashion we used to do with smoking marijuana.

The story of getting into alcohol is identical to the cycle we entered with marijuana. We would start drinking on a Tuesday night here and there. Then we started drinking on Tuesday and Thursday nights along with the typical weekend, four nights a week drinking. This routine kept progressing until, by age seventeen, we were drinking all seven nights of the week. It is as if we now had two addictions that were needed every night, marijuana and alcohol. The other narcotics were just used to add to our intoxicated state. Alcohol and marijuana became a part of our daily lives at such a young age that we were bound for two things: college and now addiction.

The Valium came into play when we could not smoke or drink, like during school. Valium is a benzodiazepine, which puts your mind in a tranquil state. We would pop a Valium and feel relaxed the entire school day. This drug did not completely capture Jayden or me, although it did enhance our carelessness. I state that it exemplifies carelessness, because you are doing drugs just to do drugs. The sole premise of doing a drug is just to do it, because "why not?" We simply were just seducing ourselves with substances whenever possible, however possible, with whomever possible.

Even though the Valium did not leave a great impact, Vyvanse indirectly impacted my addiction and carelessness more than anything. It was a solution, or quick fix, when my body was dying out and I was lifeless from the other drugs. The Vyvanse was a pick-me-up, and I utilized (or abused) the crap out of it to stay up through the school day. I would be so lifeless in the morning from getting hammered every night of the week.

We were up till peaking hours of the night, running from police at least twice a week, causing destruction, and being the neighborhood terrorizers that were bound to get arrested. We were destructive seventeen-year-olds, and with alcohol had no conscience. We destroyed neighborhoods and the community. We would be up till 4:00 a.m. throwing people's lawn furniture in the middle of the road, starting fights, knocking mailboxes over, or ripping fences apart. We had a way not to get caught, which was to run. We would run, climb fences, and use the backwoods that we knew extremely well to get away from civilians who spotted us, and even legal authorities. Once we finally got back to Jayden's residence, we knew we had to be up for school in three hours. How was this possible? That is easy…with more substances.

Vyvanse sure as hell did the trick. Vyvanse is amphetamine prescribed by the government. People feed these pills to the youth having no idea what it is. It literally "cracks you out," and is a very powerful upper. It would keep us up for nearly eighteen hours after drinking all night. Not just did it keep you up, but it also made you more focused than you would ever be without it. For me, it is like the real-life *Limitless* pill. It is an ADD medication for individuals with concentration problems; therefore, if your attention span is fine without any need for medical intervention it will put you in a state of concentration overload. If you have never heard of Vyvanse, another common drug that you may have heard of that has similar effects is Adderall.

This was amazing and contributed heavily to my addiction(s) for several reasons. First of all, it made me focus more. It actually improved my grades. It made me not care that I was intoxicated, because my grades were not being affected. It also kept you up till late that night, essentially making it possible to party all over again. This was now a daily routine I learned to adapt to, and quite frankly I loved my new life and persona. Many addicts will use Adderall, Vyvanse, and other amphetamines/methamphetamine derivatives to keep their responsibilities and addiction(s) going simultaneously. This is true especially for functioning addicts such as myself. We were picking up addictions left and right. I wish we could have made it stop in the near future, but it kept progressing.

I started getting careless about life itself. I started running on a cycle that consisted of: Vyvanse, Valium, drinking, smoking, and, sometimes, street-made substances, depending on the availability on a daily basis. This cycle tuned me into a state of autopilot, and made me develop a careless attitude toward life. After trying marijuana, alcohol, ecstasy, opiates (Vicodin), benzodiazepines (Valium), and amphetamines (Vyvanse) we thought of a new experiment – the hallucinogen. Hallucinogens were the last experiment we had.

Hallucinogens were the last experiment we had. They instilled the fear of the unknown. The ambiguity comes from the fact that everyone has different experiences that range from horrible to wonderful "trips." With downers you know you will be mellow, and with uppers you can assume you will be abnormally alert. When shrooms and LSD came to our small town of Virginia, our peers just described it as "tripping." We were clueless about what "tripping" meant, and curiosity was starting to eat us alive. We were advised to try shrooms first, because they were less potent than LSD. The dilemma was money. The currency needed to support our addiction to drugs was getting out of control.

Luckily, at this point we were selling a larger quantity of marijuana, so the marijuana was free. We would just sell enough so we no longer had to support this habit, which saved us a couple hundred dollars a week each. We would sell in order to smoke for free and we would use our profit to increase our inventory. Now we were at the point where we could spend that money on other things, primarily other drugs. With that said, we finally had the financial backing to buy a good amount of shrooms. The first time we tried them was on a Tuesday night. This is also an example of our carelessness. I say this because we were doing them on a school night with no worries regarding the repercussions. If worst comes to worst, I could always rely on a forged doctor's note and skip school, I thought to myself. We bought an eighth and split it, leaving us with 1.75 grams each to eat.

They were gold and tasted absolutely awful. It was absolutely worth it, despite the disgusting taste. This experience was like no other drug. Forty-five minutes after we ingested the shrooms, the walls started breathing, dimensions of the apartment seemed they were changing, and we were without a doubt hallucinating. We continued to munch on them every couple weeks or so. Our buddy Steven would also become a part of the hallucinating festivities with us. Remember, peer pressure again presented itself in the situation.

When we explained to him what it was like, curiosity got to him as it had with us. The three amigos (Jayden, Steven, and myself) had a blast hallucinating. I fell in love with this unlike with any other drug. At seventeen years old, I found out that I love hallucinating more than any other feeling an alternative drug can give me. I thought so abstractly, and my vision was just as altered as my thoughts. This was my new poison of choice. I woke up the next morning like my life had changed.

It was not long, about three days, before we decided to try LSD. We each took two hits. This had a similar but amplified effect as the shrooms did. The LSD had a couple differences, my favorite being the amplified abstract thinking. Shrooms gave me more of a body and visual trip, but what I loved was the altering of your psyche and mental state. I thought about the universe, and I even would come up with theories that were unheard of.

For example, I thought what if life was just a brain. All the people in this brain are simply brain cells. The one percent are the strongest brain cells, the ninety-nine percent are essentially regular brain cells, and the psychopaths are malfunctioning brain cells. Then inside your brain is another planet "earth" with the same characteristics. Your brain, and the cells, are just another society like ours. This is a crazy theory that seemed so likely on the drug... I thought of scenarios similar to that one every time I was on LSD, which became extremely frequent. My personality and drug tendencies found the LSD, and unfortunately I had fallen in love. Out of all the poisons I had experimented with this was by far my favorite...I adored LSD.

Senior year came around, and we had tried every drug available on the market. We had experimented heavily with cocaine, LSD, shrooms, painkillers, benzos, MDMA, ecstasy, and, of course, copious amounts of alcohol and marijuana. Before Jayden and I knew it, we were known as the school druggies, and we loved it. Some of them were street drugs, others were prescription, and some were over the counter, such as Nyquil. We would even steal over-the-counter cough syrup to extract the DXM (the active "robotrip" chemical) by putting the syrup in distilled water. The fact of the matter is, we tried just about everything. Furthermore, everything we tried we ended up loving. What else can you expect from an addict?

Marijuana and alcohol stayed with us. In fact, all it did was become part of our daily necessities. Everything I did my senior year I was high on something, even lacrosse games. Driving I was under the influence, eating I was under the influence, school I was under the influence, and even work I was under the influence – literally every day, all day. More and more friends followed this road, but Jayden and I were by far the worst. People knew to call us for whatever they needed, and we could get it to them. We felt accomplished by these titles that contributed to our false reality.

A couple months into senior year, my metaphoric "abuser" "hit" me for the first time. We were in Greenville, Virginia, hanging out with a large group of individuals. Jayden and I were in my '86 Camaro. I had bought this Camaro for twelve hundred dollars due to the fact that it was not stock, and barely even street legal. It was a V8355 carb that was on slicks. The interior was gutted so it was at a minimal weight to optimize its potential speed. I loved racing, and as you know, I also loved ecstasy.

We were leaving the Greenville shopping center's parking lot when a Mustang next to us was revving the engine. I looked at Jayden at the red light we were stopped at with a smirk of readiness. His look back was almost the complete opposite; he looked concerned for our safety. He usually was always ready for anything, but his nerves were wrecked due to the fact that I was under the influence of the MDMA. Once the light turned green, my foot slammed on the gas pedal. My vehicle blew past the opponent without an issue, but there was a bigger issue at hand...I was so out of it, my foot felt too heavy to lift off the gas pedal. We were racing towards the ditch as Jayden screamed, "Dude! The race is F**KING over! Stop!" I closed my eyes in a panic, but Jayden had enough reality left inside him to yank on the emergency break, causing us to spin out. Thanks to Jayden we eventually came to a safe stop. To most people this would be a reality slap, but to an addict it is simply a funny story.

I did an array of wild things that should have been a reality slap, including car chases, drug robberies, and other illegal activities. All of these actions were against my sober conscience, but with drugs I had lost all sense of that. I had broken into houses and business establishments, been involved in physical altercations, and lived a life based on edge and danger. I will not elaborate too much, but there is one incident that I really should have learned from, but of course didn't. If the law, societal morals, and fear of injury didn't stop you, you'd think a near-death experience would, right? Wrong.

It was a week before finals and we were celebrating a friend's birthday. We started the festivities the night before his birthday and continued them extremely early before school that next day. I had been up extremely late, therefore only getting three hours of rest, maximum. With that said, I took 120 mg of Vyvanse (a typical dose prescribed to Jayden was thirty mg). After the Vyvanse kicked me back into gear, Jayden and I met up with our friend to smoke, and we smoked a lot. We smoked four blunts with Logan that had eight Percocet divided between all of them. Everyone was so stoned that the last two were split between Logan and I. This is nearly two grams of marijuana, two Percocet, and 120 mg of Vyvanse that I consumed singlehandedly. I felt strange, and concentrating in my first and second class was nearly impossible. I was sweating profusely, my vision was blurred and I was nearly having an out-of-body experience.

I was dozing out of consciousness in my third block class when I finally passed out with my head slamming on the desk. I slept in class nearly every day so my teacher did not see anything too unusual until she noticed nothing was waking me up. My peers were screaming my name and vigorously shaking my body, receiving no reaction from me. I was speed balling. My heart did not know whether to speed up or slow down, so it simply malfunctioned. I shut my eyes to ignore the pain, and ended up going unconscious, having no sense of my surroundings. Nathan, a peer of mine, finally slammed a book right next to my ear, accidently hitting the side of my head. My head instantly sprang up, seeing everyone in the classroom directing their attention at me.

The teacher then walked me to the nurse's office to rest on the bed the school provided for me. I gained a bit of consciousness to tell the nurse I had texted my father. I stated he was outside. This was all a complete lie; I was going to attempt to walk back to Jayden's and pass out before anyone found out what was actually going on. I walked out the doors of my high school and stumbled all the way back to Jayden's residence, where I would sleep for fifteen consecutive hours. All of my friends had heard about what had happened at lunch, and Jayden informed them I was able to snake my way out of it. I am convinced the only reason the teacher did not report the incident is because I was days away from graduating. Nonetheless, I got off scot-free.

More and more of our friends participated in this drug lifestyle, even though most of them just smoked. They were having a fun time while they were young, but by no means were addicts. When it came down to the harder drugs, Jayden, Steven, and I typically did them. Marijuana consumed all of our friends, though – believe it or not, even Stephanie. If you recall from earlier in the book, Stephanie hated all drugs with a passion, including marijuana. We all lived our senior year blazing up and drinking together like many high-school groups of friends, but our friends did not know they were doing it with two addicts that had not realized they were full-blown addicted quite yet.

This lifestyle continued until graduation, and guess what – we were intoxicated. I had smoked and ingested a significant amount of Valium before we took the ride to Old Dominion University for our high-school graduation ceremony. Once we got there, I took Valium awaiting graduation. I was obviously under the influence on stage, because the conductors of the graduation looked at me as if they knew I was under the influence. I believe to this day they only let it slide due to the fact that they figured I would be out of their hair for good in a few hours. Regardless, somehow, I was able to proceed in my ceremony, getting off the hook scot-free once again.

We threw our hats up in the air, and got the "good lucks" from everyone. After the graduation ceremony we got plastered on the beach, and we started to reminisce about our high school years. I just thought of all the drugs I did, and how I was going to leave it all behind after that night. It was almost as if I was mourning giving up drugs instead of celebrating the fact that we were moving on to the next chapter in our life. Maybe that is why I went so crazy during the concluding weeks of high school, because I knew it was all coming to a screeching halt as I entered the adult world, losing all of my drug connections.

Stephanie, Steven, and a couple other friends and I sat on the beach, where we smoked, popped pills, and drank until the sun started to rise. Jayden had plans to go to Radford University, and Stephanie was also attending school at Kingsdale University. I also had several other good friends going off to school in other states. My friend Davis was going to Florida, and my friend by the name of Ricky decided he was going to East Carolina University. Steven decided to attend Tidewater, which was the local community college. Everyone seemed to have a route, including myself.

Soon my time with Jayden would diminish as my one-way flight to LAX approached. My new town would be the fast-paced rat race known as Los Angeles. I would soon be living with my mother and two sisters. We continued to get incredibly intoxicated until the night I left for California. It was a sad time, but I figured it would get my head on straight due to the fact that I couldn't be so under the influence in front of my mother and sisters.

Life was now about being in the criminal justice field at Pierce College. I felt lucky that I would be leaving with my hands free of any trouble with parents, the law, or my health. I figured the sober life that consisted of rules, regulations, and guidelines was coming whether I was ready or not. I came to the realization that I would have to leave the fantasy lifestyle behind, and I was entering the sober (normal) population. It sucked to come to that actualization… I left days after we graduated, said bye to my old friends, and figured I was saying hello to sobriety…real world, here I come. At least I thought that was the case, but I moved west while my addiction moved south.

VI.
Different Locality, Same Mentality

"THE EXPLANATION"

BEFORE I CONTINUE MY PERSONAL story in Los Angeles, I need to thoroughly explain two more aspects of addiction and the complexity that accompanies it. You have comprehended peer pressure, loss of innocence, justification, comparison, and everything in between. Let's add more layers to the complexion cake. This chapter will portray two more characteristics of addiction. The first feature is more of a misconception than an attribute. People often believe that moving an addict to a new geological area will tarnish the addiction. Try to compare addiction to an illness. OH WAIT! Addiction *is* an illness.

Imagine if you have cancer and believe that if you move to Texas, it will magically go away. No way, that sounds ridiculous. You may receive better treatment and resources to assist you, but regardless, you will still have the cancer when you arrive. Locality change is almost irrelevant; the addict's mind must change to resolve the problem. The mind has to move into a better place, not the physical body. The moving tactic may be possible, but it will only be effective if the addict finds new networks, new resources, and an entirely new outlook on life. Moving to a different area is a temporary fix to a permanent problem. The problem is just masked for the time being and it will not take long to show itself again.

If you move to a different locality, you find a house, grocery stores, jobs, and gas stations relatively quickly. This is essentially because these are all necessities for an individual, or it is difficult to live without. Whether you realize it or not, you naturally attract yourself to these necessities. With that said, the individual who needs their substance will find it quickly. Whether they have faced realization or not, it is a necessity in their mind that they are consciously, and unconsciously, thinking about on a regular basis.

The second trait I need to elaborate on is the addiction characteristic of carelessness. Carelessness is a feature of addiction that is the key to plummeting to the rock bottom. When this trait kicks in, you can consider yourself at optimal speed toward your rock bottom. I started to explain how carelessness pertains to addiction in previous sections, but I did not express this in nearly enough detail. It is incumbent to know how much it factors into losing a grip on reality. The addict will become careless of their relationships, consequences, and overall well-being. Addiction deepens more with carelessness than with justification and comparison combined. I feel it is a necessity to understand carelessness to understand an addict.

The definition of carelessness is as follows:

1. Taking insufficient care; negligent.
2. Marked by or resulting from lack of forethought or thoroughness.
3. Showing a lack of consideration.
4. Unconcerned or indifferent; heedless: careless of the consequences.

Doing drugs is careless within itself, but when addiction deepens so does the magnitude of carelessness. If you are a fifteen-year-old smoking into a "spoof" (which is a dryer sheet rubber banded to a toilet paper/paper towel roll) to mask the smell, this is proof you still care about the consequences. If there is a level of caring, you are not being careless in the truest form. An addict, believe it or not, comes to a point where they literally could not care less about their consequences. Let us go one by one through the definitions of carelessness and explain how they pertain to addiction.

1. **Negligence** – Addiction can force neglecting other responsibility-ies such as work or family.
2. **Lack of forethought** – Addicts do not think of long-term repercussions of their actions.
3. **Lack of consideration** – Addicts will not take into consideration how often they are using a substance. An alcoholic will say, "So I drink, so does 70% of America." They are disregarding the fact that they are drinking a 750ml bottle in one sitting on a daily basis.
4. **Carelessness of consequence** – Do you recall when I stated addicts can only see the small picture? Essentially, they see the moment. They cannot see further than using the substance. They cannot comprehend consequences that loved ones try to force down their throat until the consequences slap them in the face during the moment they are happening.

All the aspects of carelessness intertwine, leaving the addict without a care in the world. I guess they have one concern, and that is being under the influence with their poison of choice. People cannot comprehend how their child used to care about life's entirety and then suddenly have no care. The mind has not changed naturally; on the contrary, their metaphorical abuser has changed it for them. The feeling, and, even more so, the chemical, morphs the addict into a different person. The person on drugs is now careless, and the drugs caused that. The carelessness makes the individual want more drugs. It is a terrifying cycle that blankets the addict's true thoughts, morals, and life as a whole. This vicious cycle will inevitably contribute to the "abuser's" effects on addiction and the addict's well-being.

Let us use another example with cursing. When you are eight you rarely curse, if at all. When you are thirteen maybe you curse in certain instances, or even certain words. For example, maybe you will say damn or piss, but you would never say the "F word." At the age of eighteen, your mouth may have no filter. This precisely how carelessness is for addiction. An addict will start with no drugs, and a significant amount of thoughtfulness in their actions. When the world starts changing around them, they might try marijuana, but would never even contemplate doing a narcotic. In time, this same mindset can alter to become completely careless regarding the intake of harder drugs. Before an individual can even spot this change happening they could be doing several drugs, several times a day, with no care in the world.

So what does this do to addiction? It simply is a justification. In fact, this is the most simplistic justification you can possibly use. It is the justification that comes into play when no other justification is applicable. It is as easy as saying, "I do not care." Once you have this mindset, you have dived to rock bottom. This is the point where you can expect anyone to end up in one of those three places mentioned in the beginning of the book: the judicial system, the hospital, or six feet below the surface. Once again, this is the worst mindset an addict can obtain. This is something that people often misconstrue, or abruptly ignore, and IS THE WORST CHARACTERISTIC OF ADDICTION. At first, the individual cares. In fact, that is the exact reason they claim not to. You continue to claim you "don't care," and like everything else, if you hear that enough you will start to believe it…you believe your own lie.

Just to reiterate, the person who obtains this careless characteristic will not recover by doing something as simple as relocating. I am clueless as to how people think such a simple solution will work if addiction is as complex as it is. I too fell for this misconception, due to the denial I was in. My point is, a person will find their poison of choice anywhere if they search hard enough. Priorities for a human being are food, shelter, healthcare, and social standings. Addicts can also add their metaphorical "abuser" to this list of priorities. Essentially, an addict will find their drug as easily as you would find food. If their mind is constantly pondering the substance, the law of attraction will inevitably give it to them.

You can assume searching for the "next high" is usually taken in a figurative manner, but this is not always true. You can also mean this literally. Like I said previously, if a person is looking for the next figurative high (meaning the next level of influence), they will not stop until it is found, and the same goes for the literal meaning. If someone is trying to find the next high literally (finding another dosage), they will not stop until they get what they want. This is ingrained in their personality, their addictive biological predisposition. In conclusion, relocation will essentially put an addict on a literal search for their next high. If an addict has hit their carelessness point of addiction, relocation will not make a difference. Typically, a complex problem calls for a sophisticated solution, and by now you see addiction is an extremely complex problem. It is sad how parents move, or relocate the addict, and still come short of recovery.

You must comprehend how dangerous the carelessness mindset is. This aspect of addiction will increase the addiction's severity significantly. When the drug has convinced you that there are no worries in the world but the drug, you will focus more and more time on this metaphorical "abuser." This must be caught immediately, because it happens subconsciously at such an incredibly fast rate.

This chapter will continue to explain and expand on my personal addiction. I will demonstrate with my real-life journey how relocation will not solve the problems of addiction. I will proceed to prove every point I have made in this introduction, and therefore better your understanding on the subjects of carelessness and relocation. These two aspects are not necessarily simultaneous, as with justification and comparison, but they did happen to enter my journey during the same era of addiction.

"I MOVED WEST, MY ADDICTION MOVED SOUTH"

MY MIND WAS REMINISCING ABOUT the older days. I was consistently in a mindset in which I was reliving the times of high school, and of course all of the substance consumption. I'd lost everything I had, and I needed to rebuild in a completely different society. I arrived at LAX in Los Angeles after a full day of traveling, where my mother's smile glistened when she appeared at the top of the escalator leading to the baggage claim. My hindsight was already activated, thinking whether I had made a mistake moving back out to the West Coast. I walked outside to enormous buildings, several billboards, and numerous metro areas blanketing the entire city. The new environment of being back in the city excited me, although I felt a pit of emptiness from leaving Jayden and my party days behind.

No doubt, I was more depressed than excited about leaving my old life and starting a new chapter. I was forced to leave all of my friends, my life, and my nights of intoxication behind. I was terrified of having to rebuild new networks, job opportunities, and the mental mind-state of adulthood, more specifically sobriety. The thought of being sober every day was dreadful and caused severe anxiety. This is an outlook shared by all addicts. I thought it would be easy, but it was the most difficult dilemma that I had ever encountered. I figured I "really, really, really" wanted it, but did not need it.

Remember what I said regarding this: you may think you really only want it – a very false statement. This is just another contribution to a false reality. The pathetic truth was that I needed substances, and I had no grasp of that fact until my resources for the substances had vanished. I had used justification at such an excessive rate that I thought I could "easily quit whenever I want." I continued to say that, even though my actions completely contradicted that.

I was rummaging through ideas to find a connection to any substance that would take me out of the depressing state of sobriety. I had no connections whatsoever. I was falling into a dark state of withdrawals leading to depression all because I had "broken up with my abuser." I was in a sober drought for nearly a week, and started wondering if I had made a huge mistake. Of course, sober or not, I had to leave my life behind me, but that included the drugs. I was feeling mass amounts of anxiety about just being sober on a continual basis. I knew no one but loved ones, and I would nervously have thoughts of asking them to buy me alcohol.

It started with a couple forty-ounce beers just so I could relax my mind. I would force sympathy on them by complaining about how hard it was leaving my friends. I would manipulate them to get the substance for me, and I felt no remorse. It is common for addicts to manipulate in order to get their poison of choice; they will even manipulate loved ones. In this situation that was what I needed to do. My loved ones would not buy me alcohol if I told them, "Yes... I need this, because my anxiety is off the charts due to a sober lifestyle." I was not drinking for fun, or even because I wanted to, but because I needed to discontinue my drought.

Once the couple beers were bringing my tolerance level back up to par, I knew I needed more. I would use more manipulation to get more intoxicated. I told my loved ones that I wanted to start getting half-gallon bottles, because it would save money. The basic philosophy that buying in bulk will save the consumer money is true, but it is not the reason I wanted the half-gallon bottle. If I got the biggest bottle on the market, I would have it whenever I wanted to consume it. My loved ones were feeling guilty about enabling me to drink, and would hesitate more and more every time I asked. The hesitation made me nervous that I would not be able to get intoxicated, and that is why I would get the half-gallon bottles. A bottle lasted me three or four days, when the beer would only last me a single night.

I would try my hardest to conserve the bottles, although my tolerance was reaching to where it was when I was drinking with

Jayden. Before I knew it, I was finishing a half gallon of Svedka vodka in as little as twenty-four hours, forty-eight hours maximum. I had eventually drunk my whole savings away, and before the summer was over, I had blown more than two thousand dollars on alcohol. I had no care about money, family, or where my life was going because alcohol made all of those stressors go away. When I ran out of money to fund my addiction I would beg my loved ones, and their responses were all similar to "get a job," but they would continue to buy me alcohol. I was looking for a job with minimal effort, but now that my substance abuse had ceased due to money I put all my efforts into making more money.

We had a trip planned to visit Las Vegas, my good ol' hometown. I figured I would use this as a week to apply for jobs, and hopefully pull one in. We stayed at my uncle Darrell's house, and I thought it would be a great time to set out my options and reestablish myself in the new society I found myself in. I was excited to apply for jobs, even though I was going to have to be sober. The first couple days of the trip I was sober, but had a feeling that would change soon.

Darrell looked strung out, and I knew where the look derived from: painkillers. My family has horrendous addictive traits, and their poison of choice in Las Vegas was painkillers. I was on a little binge of painkillers myself, reverting back to the times that Logan and I had. I figured I was older and it was family, so no crisis would happen, as it had in high school.

I was applying for jobs the entire time I was "slumped" (a common phrase for the high on painkillers). The Vegas trip consisted of my mother gambling and me doing drugs. Even though I was heavily intoxicated during my little corrupted vacation, I had applied to over fifty places. I may have promised myself I wouldn't start doing narcotics again, but I was still being productive so I justified it. My excuses for my abuser had, sure enough, started again. At the time, I saw no issue due to the fact that I was doing them with family, and I was being productive in my attempts to enter early adulthood.

After a long hot summer, I finally found employment toward the end; I found a job at my local Starbucks. It was a Starbucks located in the Sherman Oaks Galleria right off of Ventura Blvd. It was in the heart of Los Angeles! A busy rat-race of wildness that I would soon be in the center of. I was practically working full time before I knew it. Tim Allen, Josh Peck, and other impactful individuals knew this Starbucks as their local coffee shop. It was an opportunity that filled my head with overwhelming excitement.

I only had two days off, and those were my days I would be attending school at Pierce College once it was in session. School was coming up right around the corner. Ironically, I was studying criminal justice. I was anxious to develop networks there as I was doing at Starbucks. I knew that I would meet an array of people to hang out, build relationships, and of course do drugs with. I had already met a couple people, but none that were too resourceful in regards to finding my poisons. These friends at Starbucks faded away due to the fact that they were not into the same thing I was – which was substance abuse. I just saw them as "law-abiding conformers." I did not get to know them all that well, but by a brief personality evaluation I figured they had no intentions of living the lifestyle I was.

The mindset I had was asinine, but I was a criminal justice major and working full time; there was nothing anyone could tell me. I was doing something good that most people don't: going to college. I sure as hell continued using this as justification for my addiction, and it made perfect sense to an addict.

"I am doing fine; I am furthering my education and working full time. What is the big deal about altering my mind state with substances here and there? I am an adult now; I can make my own decisions."

Not only did I use this to justify my addiction, but I also used it to justify that addiction to my loved ones. I would inform them on a daily basis how great I was doing in life, and they had no right to judge or try to reprimand me for drinking when I got home. This manipulation benefited my metaphorical abuser, because my family did not even want to argue with me regarding my polysubstance addiction issues. This could be because it would always end up in a horrific verbal argument. My mom continued to feel bad for me, soaking up my manipulating behavior, which continually worked.

With that said, she knew that someone my age lived next door named Philip. He was older than I was but still living at home with his father, although his head seemed to be on straight. He was a very respectful guy to my mother. She let him know that she now had an eighteen-year-old kid that lived in the household. She thought it would be good for me to meet this respectful young man, and she proceeded to give him my number. He informed her that when he got off work he would give me a call to come hang out. Initially I was not too excited, but since I had nothing else to do I figured I would get to know my new neighbor.

My timid knock on the door was loud enough for a middle-aged man to acknowledge as he proceeded to open the door. The man seemed confused about why I had brought myself to the residence. Twenty-four-year-old Philip brushed himself past the middle-aged man to introduce himself. He used his body language to welcome me into his house. As I was walking in, I was simultaneously giving a farewell gesture to my mother as she looked indecisive. I could not tell if she was happy or worried. Philip did not look like a well-brought-up guy once she saw him in his casual clothes. He lived in the same rundown project-looking apartment building I did in the local county of Sherman Oaks. He had several tattoos consisting of crests, lions, and a large marijuana symbol that covered his left shoulder. He was obviously stoned a majority of his day. Within minutes, it was no secret that he partied just as much as I did; my mom just prayed he would be a good influence and not further my addiction.

I walked into Philip's room, and it depicted the California stoner mentality perfectly. Covering the walls were posters of *Alice in Wonderland* and Marilyn Monroe, and drug propaganda bombarded the tiny room. His bookshelves consisted of no books, but instead there were cartoon DVD series, memorabilia action figures, and pictures of parties. It looked like Jayden's attic transformed into a small bedroom. He had steamrollers, bongs, bowls, glass shards, grinders, and other paraphernalia surrounding the premises of his room. Covering the dressers were bottles of liquor and other drug-related items. As my eyes meandered around the room, I knew I'd met someone with similar interests – being under the influence. As the months went by, I continued to get more and more intoxicated with Philip. We became very close as time went on. We were habitually hanging out –as Jayden and I had.

Philip was barely twenty-four when I first moved to California, and I was barely a legal adult. During the first few weeks I would drink and smoke with Philip at his pace. Roughly fourteen to twenty shots and countless bowls later, I noticed we were on two different levels. When I was highly intoxicated I was willing to go out, drive, and be energetic, and I felt a sense of readiness toward several other dangerous activities I should not do while that intoxicated. Philip would much rather play it safe. He would just fade into a deep sleep from the substance after hanging out watching comical shows and movies. When Philip knocked out, I would try to discreetly go back home, which was right next door. I would wake up my mother on a consistent basis with my loud entrance.

"What the hell?" my mom shouted from the other room. She woke up and stormed into the living room of our tiny one-bedroom apartment. My drunk wobble knocked over a plethora of dishes on the counter in the kitchen. The sudden loud noises mixed with the rage of my mother woke up my sister, who was thirteen at the time. When she entered the living room, she heard me yelling horrific things to my mother that I will regret till the day I die. Sydney was a beautiful thirteen-year-old-girl, and is still a saint. She has been through as much heart grief as me plus more, and would still never touch a controlled substance. She dealt with the same abusive stepfather that I had for nearly twelve years, a father committing suicide, and my mother's cancer.

Sydney looked at me with a face of disappointment and disgust. I saw agony in her eyes. The distraught look was not from me being drunk, but the hard times of despair that we'd undergone as children.

The background of addiction on my mother's side was horrendous. My grandfather recovered from heroin, my cousins were alcoholics, and even my mother did cocaine for some while. Even though these addictions are hard for a thirteen-year-old to hear, it was nothing compared to what she had seen…for example, my stepfather, Gabriel.

Gabriel made my mom, sisters, and my entire family hate alcohol – therefore, the reason my family caught on to and starting hating my alcoholic personality. What is this personality? I know it better than anyone, because I lived through the abuse and was the abuser. To understand what I saw in my sister's eyes the night she caught me that intoxicated, you would have to understand what her precious eyes had seen through her life regarding alcoholism. It wasn't her eyes that bothered me; it was the story I could symbolically see behind them.

My sister's eyes, upon seeing me in this drunken rage, told a story longer than this book in only a few brief seconds. The flashback of physical and emotional abuse was overwhelming me, and causing me to just want the shot of the whiskey sitting on the table. Her eyes told a story that started when I was just seven years old (making her three) of listening to my stepfather yelling at me in a drunken rage and screaming names including, but not limited to: faggot, fat fuck, titty boy, pussy, worthless, fat shit, tub-a-lard. The list goes on and haunts me to this day. The story her eyes projected continued on to him throwing food at her (suggesting she was fat), starting when she was as young as six. My mom did not flee this alcoholic rage we encountered. For her it was worth staying; her abuser was contaminating her mind (just like a drug). My stepfather would call her the most degrading things you could imagine: cunt, bitch, fat, ugly, old, stupid, etc. These words made her feel helpless, submissive, controlled, and worthless. Similar to how an addict feels at times.

I started racing through flashbacks of Gabriel terrorizing our family, the domestic violence calls, and the depression that my family and I suffered due to Gabriel's alcoholism. The beatings my mother got from Gabriel were catastrophes that have never faded from my memory. The cops would come to an enraged man, and then leave casually without any judicial punishment because of the forgiveness my mother would continually give. Unfortunately, it made the violence worse.

The next time I tried to call the police, which was weeks later, he threatened to kill me. Was this him being abusive because he was a psychopath, or was he just a messenger boy for his alcoholism? I am not justifying actions like this. If it is you consuming the substance, and the substance causing the actions, it is directly your fault. I am using it as another metaphor to try and understand if this was his personality, or his personality while drunk. As they say in the clichéd expression, "if you beat your wife drunk, don't drink." The problem for Gabriel, and now myself, is that being intoxicated regularly makes this personality YOU, whether you internalize that fact or not.

I would be fortunate to say that was the conclusion of what I saw in my sister's eyes, but it was only the beginning. My mind went to other death threats that could be taken more seriously. One cold December night my cousin and I were looking at Gabriel's collection of Hot Wheels when he was out in the garage pounding beers. After the second case of Natural Light, he went into his room to either puke or urinate when he noticed one of his Hot Wheels had been relocated to another crate. He knew someone had rummaged through his collection; consequently, his drunk-rage button was pushed. My cousin and I heard a rampage going on inside the house of breaking glass, rambunctious yelling, and physical force on hard objects such as walls and possibly even my mother.

We saw the six-foot-five, 350-pound savage ruthlessly swinging the back door open. My cousin and I were on the trampoline, reminiscing about our elementary school days and talking about my future plans of high school in Virginia. Our conversation was suddenly interrupted by the drunken beast. My heart stopped immediately once I saw what was in Gabriel's right hand. He was waving a shiny knife around as if it were the GED he'd never gotten. I feared for my life, thinking that night could be my last. He was drunkenly screaming for about forty-five minutes with the knife in his hand until he finally punched a hole in the wall and drove off after drinking over forty-eight beers.

I finally had a conversation with my mother, talking about what Gabriel and his alcohol was doing to the family. I'd had this conversation with my mother before, and it always led to her leaving, and then coming back. Like I have stated repeatedly, the domestic-violence cycle is identical to drugs. This time I told her, "I don't even feel bad for you or myself anymore, I feel bad for my sisters – they can't help it." These words hit so strong that my mom went to a shelter, and never went back to Gabriel. The abuse my family and I witnessed and encountered is a story within itself, and I could very well write it one day.

Anyway, I want to stay focused on addiction, assuming that is why you are reading this book. There is a main point, as well as a side point that I want to reiterate. The main point being that Gabriel and I were turning into the same person, and that is exactly what I saw in my sister's eyes. I saw my reflection in her glistening eyes, and it was Gabriel staring back at me. Metaphorically, this was the point in my life when I was "seriously done with substances, and would never go back." I refused to be a "Gabriel." I promised my mother I would quit drinking, and I truly believed I was going to. The night of emotion led me to this metaphorical breakup with my abuser.

The trends in a drug relationship, and any addict's ineffective attempt at recovery, were not any different in my situation. The cycle played out just like a woman running back to her abusive husband, just like my mom ran back to Gabriel after leaving him four times… I ran back to alcohol. I justified my actions, and that is exactly what my mother would do for Gabriel. At this point, you should have a thorough understanding of how similar drug addiction and domestic violence are, and they have never been compared…and that is my side point. Essentially, it could revolutionize addiction if DV counselors and addiction counselors worked in conjunction with one another to develop a repeatable, and more effective, solution, knowing the similarities that have never been compared before. My benefit is I have experienced both firsthand, and have seen how similar the attributes of these two crises are.

After justifying the night before, I continued the day by having my morning toke with Philip. I convinced myself that everything was all right, and I'd just had a bad night. I had an identical reaction a battered woman would have: the next morning I was trying to justify and forget. I looked to blame work, the stress of reestablishing, and even the type of liquor it was (which many people do). I didn't get intoxicated for a couple days, although I quickly whirled into the same deviant ways I'd been in before.

My mother figured it was no big deal since we only hung around next door, and only hung out with one another with no other influencers. That concept my mother had started to develop would soon be proven wrong, because she completely ignored the law of attraction – like attracts like. Before my mother could realize her mindset was bogus I was meeting people at a rapid rate who all had the same interest as I did, and that was substances. My mom claimed she was a psychic and consequently knew that I was doing drugs in Virginia, but not that I was doing them with Philip. Why wasn't I doing drugs? Was it because I didn't want to, or because I didn't have the social networks yet? The door opened to meet Philip; I met his friends, and found the people who could get me the best drugs of Los Angeles. Once again, all through the law of attraction. The relocation was a temporary fix to a permanent problem, resulting in a failed recovery.

As time went on, I met several friends I would smoke and drink with, but I also met a few people I would reach the next level with. Robert, Milley, and Morgan became my new buddies, full of danger and excitement. Cocaine, LSD, and painkillers consumed my life before I even knew what I was getting myself into. These three individuals had the same goal in mind that I did – to be more intoxicated than the night before...

Robert was a twenty-four-year-old fast-paced guy who glistened with charisma. He grew up in Australia, and went to UCLA to experience America. In Australia, he developed a terrible habit of cocaine, and consequently dropped out of UCLA. The coke had gotten the best of him. When he was not on the drug he was hyped up on coffee, and ironically he worked at Starbucks with me. He developed a personality from the drug, a false power of being ecstatic nearly twenty hours a day. His persona was full of life, especially when he was high. The ego made him reminiscent of the Mask as played by Jim Carey. A ladies' man, thin, attractive, sharp, witty, full of life, and the type of guy who makes people think, "I want to be him. He optimized these characteristics as an entertainer on the side.

The best part was he would always bring me along. He seemed on top of the world, and this made me strive to feel like that. These traits he had were not necessarily socially or biologically developed, but were instilled chemically. Logically, I could easily grasp these traits with a little poison. Cocaine was his rush, and he glistened with an abnormal amount of life when he was with this metaphorical abuser. Now, I keep saying him, but you share many interests as friends, especially when the two friends are addicts. Essentially, this was me in the making as well. Obviously, Robert was a bad influence. The mutual influence on each other became worse and worse. One night we were blown out of our mind for hours touring Ventura Boulevard, and I passed out on a couch in a hotel lobby. Robert was far from done. Once Robert finished his nightly fun, we were on the way to drop me back off at my apartment. That is, until a high-speed chase occurred in a '99 Mercedes owned by Robert Canton.

"We have a '99 black Mercedes going 105 mph on Ventura Blvd, need back up."

I was the passenger seat in this pursuit, springing wide awake and terrified. This is one of many incidents when drugs almost destroyed me and my loved ones' lives. No problem to an addict; as usual, I would just justify it later. The chase ended out of the fear of Robert having a heart attack or crashing; consequently my friend pulled over. He ingested the rest of his Cocaine before he came to a complete stop. The officer charged Robert with fleeing the authority, and eventually drove me home to tell the crew the tragic ending to a great night.

I came home to inform Philip how Robert had just gone insane, and felt as if he was untouchable to the law, the country, and even life itself. I couldn't fathom it. Philip proceeded to explain why if you do use a substance you have to be smart, or at least show some care. This should have been enough for any person to stop the drug usage. Although an addict is not any regular human being.

I enjoyed hanging out with the clan after work even after the event, especially on the weekend. We would take bumps off of a spoon the size of a pea. The 8-ball would slowly be dented, and after three small lines or so at a time we would go to the bar. Ordering younger than twenty-one was fairly common in Los Angeles, more so than someone who is not from the area would expect. The demand of certain bars made the extra time it takes to check IDs a nuisance and would slow down the flow of business significantly.

The lifestyle I was living continued, and got worse with more drugs. Robert was all about his cocaine, but you could say we were a diverse group of addicts. Milley reintroduced me to my poison of choice, LSD. LSD enhanced my senses and mind, and I loved that more than anything else in my life. I remember all my trips, and I am going to go through the ones that will be important further along my road to recovery. I don't recount my trips to brag or give a description of what enough acid can do, but because you will find the information very important toward the conclusion of the story. With that said, I will briefly describe these trips solely for you to be able to reference them later in the book.

The LSD we got was pure, and was always dropped on our tongue. Imagine an eye drop container, and the drops falling into your eyes. This is identical to the process of taking LSD, but rather than dropping them in the eye, you drop them on your tongue. This "hit" typically cost around ten dollars per drop. LSD users commonly prefer this over the alternative option, which is a pre-dropped "hit" on a tiny piece of dissolvable paper. Milley had a boyfriend who was one of the largest LSD dealers in the valley. We would always do it for free; consequently, we would do the LSD a lot more than we probably should have. Although LSD is not the sole drug I used, I became addicted to the trips it provided more than anything.

My first hard trip occurred in Milley's new place. She had just moved into a suburb of Burbank with her new boyfriend. Milley and her boyfriend decided to try his new batch of LSD. This LSD had an extraterrestrial effect to it. The reaction was remarkable; no other drug could make you see or feel like that. I dropped six hits on my tongue, and within an hour I started tripping relatively hard. Everything became animated or cartoonish looking. Milley's face started to become smooth, and her boyfriend seemed to start looking like an animated Disney character of some sort. As the trip progressed, I decided to go and lie down due to the anxiety it was causing me, the anxiety that I loved for some reason.

I stepped over a large mirror that was on the floor right next to the bed. The mirror was on the floor because they had just moved into the new apartment. I struggled to lie on my side, and continued to roll onto my stomach toward the end of the bed. The covers on the bed engulfed me as if it were feeding. I was attempting to find the position that would release some of the overwhelming anxiety. I looked directly at the ground where the mirror was. I saw myself forming into a cartoon in the mirror, and I was staring at my animated self. The cartoon version of myself got stuck in my head, even after the trip. He looked just like me, except he was smaller and animated. It was almost as if Matt Stone and Trey Parker (the *South Park* creators) had drawn a sketch of me.

There was a stigma about this animated figure that I did not respect; he seemed to have a devilish mindset – as if he were the devil himself. This was the first time, but would not be the last, that I saw this figure. This animation was me, the evil, cruel, and careless human being I became. In the morning, I believed this cartoon was the ego I started developing. The cartoon version of myself stayed with me, and it seemed he would appear when I was on the LSD.

My next trip, I increased my intake to seven hits, although the last trip had terrified me beyond belief. Like I said, addicts do not think like individuals without the addictive personality; they will continue to do what harms their well-being. Seven hits and I lost grip of reality. I was also on several other substances, including an intake of DMT. The only way to describe it would be I entered into this portal. The only figure in this portal I spiraled into was the devilish animated figure who'd haunted me on my last trip. This trip may have spawned from my fascination with Nickelodeon cartoons, or merely from creative imagination.

This animation is something that will corrupt and taunt my mind for the rest of my life, but this specific trip made this cartoon character so real. This alter-ego cartoon was the devil in me that would change my outlook on my life, consequently leaving all my morals at the door of sobriety. This ego was no good, but I had no idea it would potentially end my sanity. I became addicted to this animation that surrounded me. Originally, this figure would only be stalking me on acid. After using LSD more frequently, the figure steadily became more relevant in my day-to-day life.

These trips continued to become more realistic, and the cartoon figure started to dominate my LSD trips. I knew this was not good, but for some reason I fell in love with the anxiety and excitement this brought to the table. As the amount of LSD increased, so did the realism of the animation. The LSD would do things to my mind such as: instill flashbacks from other trips, do things as bizarre as convincing me that my friends were going to call the police, and even give me the ability to merge and alter all five of my senses.

Merging my five senses is something that words cannot describe. When I was tripping on the LSD it was as if I could smell and hear colors, or feel a taste. For example, red was a loud and obnoxious color with a strong smell of lavender. Making your brain do something like this opens your mind in a way it can't sober, and I loved that feeling. This ultimately drove my addiction with LSD, and consequently, you could say, it was driving me insane.

The LSD trips on a consistent basis came to an end and became a weekend getaway. The only reason I was able to cut back drastically was the fact that I knew school was coming up and the LSD was seriously affecting my brain. I needed to prepare myself for my first semester of college. Pierce College was a small campus located in Woodland Hills. It almost looked like a high school. It by no means represented a "college experience." It did not meet my expectations, but I was stuck and had to make the best of what I had. I didn't know if the emptiness of satisfaction came from the nature of the school or if I just sincerely missed the peers I'd had on the East Coast.

As the summer came to a close, I knew I was going to need a vehicle since I had obligations I needed to attend all throughout the Valley. I had been taking the Metro, and I was sick and tired of it. With that said, I was able to save up 1,800 dollars and bought myself a 1991 Camaro. This enabled me to drive under the influence, which terrified my mom, but she knew I needed some way to drive to school. I also had a new spot where I could consume the drugs, which was awesome! I would utilize this before, after, and even during school. The bottom line was school was going as great as I could possibly make it, and so was work. When I say "as great as possible," it essentially means being under the influence as much as possible to ease the misery that I had buried inside me. I had finally gotten everything back and started with my new life, my new society, and my substances, but there was still something substantially missing.

School was fun, but it was not the party lifestyle I wanted. I expected big basement parties, beautiful women, and an array of drug options. Pierce College was by no means providing any of that. The worst part was I would constantly be on the phone with my high-school friends hearing how magnificent the university life was treating them. Ricky was having a good time at ECU, Stephanie was loving her time at Kingsdale, and Jayden was having a delightful experience at Radford. It seemed as if everyone loved the new chapter in their book except for me, and that was extremely hard to cope with. It is one thing hating your circumstances, but it makes it so much worse when your best friend is informing you about everything that you are missing out on. Jayden would constantly tell me how amazing the people were that he was meeting, and he suggested that I come to visit in the near future to check the university out. I wanted to see how amazing the experience was, to at least get a taste of the university life.

My first semester at Pierce College was coming to a close. Phone calls between Jayden and I had become more frequent due to the fact that I wanted to find a way to visit Radford. I had now been in Los Angeles for about eight months, and once everything was settled I still felt depressed. I do not know if it was because I lived in a one-bedroom apartment with four people, or if it was the fact that I was back under a parent's supervision. Parental rules and regulations were something that hadn't existed for the past three years. I was unhappy, and a trip to visit Jayden was exactly what I needed as a morale booster. I wanted to get out and live the college experience, at least for a weekend or so. When talking to friends, I would tell them how wonderful Los Angeles was, but the truth was I hated it...I wanted to see if the grass was truly greener on the other side.

Being upset with my life accompanied by everyone loving theirs got me thinking. I thought maybe I don't want to go visit Jayden, but just need to go to a university. The only thing that was stopping me was my four-year plan (two years at Pierce followed by two years at a UC school). My GPA was a 3.6 and my SAT scores were in the top thirty percent of my school, but the academic plan I had set out for myself would be voided if I were to start at a university in the near future. I would no longer be able to continue working on my set plan. Contradicting that issue, I could not fathom living under supervision and scrutiny for another two years. Most addicts do not want the scrutiny. Essentially, they want to do what they want without any advice or intervention. This was obviously something I couldn't get while living under my mother's roof, since she rightfully scrutinized me every day.

This got me thinking about changing that visit to Radford to an enrollment. Besides the fact that I was in the four-year plan, another big issue was the fact that I was a week from finishing my fall semester at Pierce. Wanting to attend Radford University that spring put me in a major time crunch.

This only gave me about three weeks. My first step would be talking to Jayden about it so he could set me up with the application, information about the campus, and statistics I was unable to retrieve online. I needed to do all of this through Jayden rather than going to visit due to the fact I was 3,000 miles away and only had about three weeks to get everything squared away. A typical prospective student would go visit the campus and then attend the following year in the fall, but an addict is an extremely sporadic thinker in the "now or never" mindset. They are not just sporadic, but also talented at acquiring what they want when they want it.

I called Jayden to tell him the exciting change in my mindset. I informed him all about my idea of somehow getting enrolled at Radford. He didn't think there was enough time, but sure as hell loved the idea. He sent me all of the links I needed. He even told all of his Radford friends that the guy he talked so much about would actually be attending! He was so excited that he was willing to do anything to assure the both of us that when he departed back to Radford I would be right there with him. We saw the image of the two best friends reuniting and knew we would do anything in our power to make that image become a reality. I had already gotten a one-way ticket to Virginia to visit, but was unsure if everything was going to work out regarding admission, financial aid, and all other aspects that accompany going to a university. Like I said, this is why most people give themselves months to plan, but an addict just does the action to await the consequence rather than prepare for it.

It was a long week between Pierce College finals and attempting to enroll at Radford. At the end of the week I received a letter stating, "ACCEPTED!" I honestly did not even read the entire letter; all I needed to see was the word "accepted." I threw the paper up in the air out of excitement and went to go celebrate with the Los Angeles crew. The days following the acceptance letter were filled with good news. The government funding went through to assist me in paying tuition, I was almost sure that the dorm had space, and had my airplane ticket printed and ready to go. I was ready to depart and start my academic career at Radford University. The only thing left to do was quit my job, sell my car, and say my goodbyes to the people who were dear to me in Los Angeles.

I put my two-week notice in, sold my car for 1100 dollars, and eventually got to make my rounds with joyful yet saddening goodbyes. The night before I left started at the bar as any typical night would. I then continued the daily routine of going to Milley's house in Burbank. After about thirty minutes of smoking with the crew her boyfriend asked me to come to his room and talk. I figured it was to give me a goodbye hit of some Lucy. I was correct, but he also had a proposition for me that I could not refuse. He was going to mail me a "we miss you card" that was actually half a poster board of LSD. He was estimating he could send me six hundred hits with one card, and only wanted 3,500 dollars. This proposition was racing through my mind without rest the entire flight back to Virginia.

It was absolutely terrifying, but at the time the reward seemed far too beneficial to decline the offer. I was coming to Radford with LSD, a lot of LSD. I had made my decision to go through with it. I slowly lost my sense of nervousness and it transitioned into an overwhelming excitement to make some easy money. My night continued with smoking, drinking, and doing a lot of cocaine with good friends. Philip and I, along with the rest of clan, hung out in the apartment courtyard till my early morning flight at 5:00 a.m. The early morning festivities concluded with us discussing the proposition I'd been offered.

After my final goodbyes, my mother and sisters sent me off to LAX, the airport that she had picked me up from nine months prior. I left with all of my belongings, a sense of excitement, a slight feeling of depression, a life sentence worth of LSD being sent to me, and of course a deepened addiction. Radford University, here I come. As I sat in my seat on the airplane I knew I was ready to start the next chapter in my book, no pun intended. I was more than ready to start executing my plan of getting back on my feet residing on the East Coast, although even as I was physically going back East my addiction continued to move in no direction except south.

V.

Egotistical and Careless

"THE EXPLANATION"

LET'S START THIS SECTION WITH a brief psychology lesson. I am no psychologist, as I have stated before, but I need to thoroughly explain one more attribute of addiction before I continue with my journey to Radford University. Freud had a philosophy regarding the personality. The personality, according to Freud, has three parts. Your personality consists of the id, the ego, and the superego. The id is the primitive and instinctive component of personality. It consists of all the inherited and instinctual traits, which includes the addictive trait. We also have the ego. According to Freud, the ego develops in order to mediate between the instinctual id, the fantasized superego, and the external real world. It is the decision-making component of personality. Ideally, the ego works by reason, whereas the id is totally instinctive. Essentially, the ego is your interpretation of how the world sees you. Freud continues by explaining that the id seeks pleasure and avoids pain, instinctively. The ego differs from the id, because the ego is concerned with consciously striving to find a realistic strategy to obtain pleasure. Finally, we have the superego. The superego consists of two systems. These two systems are the "self-fulfilling" conscience and the ideal self. These work side by side.

What does this have to do with addiction? Whether you think Freud's philosophy is right or wrong, it gives a good base to explain how the addict's invincible, narcissistic, and self-centered attitude emerges. The id is important because the addictive personality can, at least partly, be at fault for addiction. More importantly, the ego develops out of control. It develops to the point that the superego, being your ideal self, is tarnished. The ego develops a realistic strategy to gain pleasure while avoiding pain. Drugs, for the addict, are very realistic and obtainable. It requires only having a little bit of money and resources.

Furthermore, the addict can simultaneously achieve pleasure and disregard their daily pains by consuming drugs. To an ego (looking for realistic pleasure) that has lost grasp of care, drugs are the answer. Then the chemicals physically alter your brain to crave the pleasure, avoid pain, and while doing this simultaneously make the image of your "ideal self" fade away without your knowledge. Your decision-making ego takes over, which is deadly to an addict, because they base their decisions on being high. It is the easiest way to satisfy the ego, achieving pleasure and avoiding pain.

At this point in the process, it seems the mind has become self-destructive, because the superego is gone. The addict believes they cannot resurrect the good, and they are content with that while addicted to the drug. This now makes it physically impossible for the superego to successfully control the ego's deadly cravings. The addict's overpowering ego is accompanied by the disappearance of your superego, leaving an individual mentally unstable. The mixture of this results in the desire for pleasure (drugs), and the loss of an individual's ethics, values, and morals. With that said, the addict will hurt whomever and whatever they need to in order to satisfy their only conscious part to their personality, the ego.

Many people who love an addict have a hard time understanding where their child, daughter, husband, friend, etc. is coming from. Loved ones will contemplate why they cannot think clearly, why they are so apathetic, and why they are throwing their life down the drain. They will claim, "This is not him/her, what has gotten into them?" This is because this process is ignored in recovery programs. The question is not necessarily what has gotten into them, but what have they gotten rid of? The answer is simple: they have lost their ideal self, their consciousness, ultimately their superego. Their morals, dreams, and ideal self (or potential) have been consumed by the short-term-pleasure-seeking ego.

They lost the ambition and the will to strive for what they potentially can be. They have lost that ambition when they once said, "Mom/Dad, I want to be an astronaut, doctor, lawyer, like you, etc. when I grow up." When they lose their ideal self and the only personality trait that is present is the ego, it results in careless ways to achieve pleasure and avoid pain. They become apathetic to their loved ones, their future, and their life itself. Now all the addict focuses on is pleasure, which eventually can only be chemically obtained through drugs. Subconsciously, they are being controlled by the drug, which makes their mind consist of nothing but an enormous ego. This is what generates the carelessness that will leave you in the three inevitable situations: hospitalized, incarcerated, or deceased.

I needed to briefly touch on this philosophy to clearly explain how an addict's ego develops. This is something that I deem to be completely accurate, although I see room for speculation. I am no PhD, but this is another aspect that is completely ignored in a typical program such as the twelve steps. This is a philosophy of addiction that recovered addicts can relate to, but the issue is the fact that it is never thought about. If you want to understand an addict, and ultimately tarnish the drug usage, you must understand what is going on in their head. This country is trying to fix the problem of addiction, doesn't contemplate the WHY of addiction, and then expects it to work. This is simply another attribute of addiction that I deem to be important. Once again, you must understand addiction to save you or a loved one from the disease.

To understand the rest of my journey, you must understand two more characteristics of addiction. Firstly, the simultaneous phenomenon of growing an ego while diminishing a superego. Secondly, the way this phenomenon develops the attribute of carelessness. Ultimately, this is when direct intervention is needed before something terrible occurs. Now that I have touched on these aspects I will demonstrate my journey, and how my road to rock bottom is no exception. Once the ego takes over, you have reached the door to rock bottom, and you will hit the solid pit at any given moment. I myself had an ego that was growing rapidly, my ideal-self vanished, and this ultimately led to my death sentence.

"ENROLLING AT RADFORD UNIVERSITY"

I FOUND MYSELF BACK IN THE beautiful state of Virginia after a long, nerve-racking flight. My father met me there with a glistening smile similar to my mother's when I had arrived in Los Angeles. It was a time to rejoice; I was rejuvenated, ecstatic, and could not wait another second to go see Jayden, Stephanie, and the rest of my high-school network. Most academic institutions were enjoying their winter break; therefore, everyone was visiting Ridge Run. It was an opportunity to reunite with friends, families, and, of course, our poisons of choice. All I could think about as my father and I were leaving the parking garage at Norfolk's National Airport was the fact that in a couple short hours, I would be back with everything and everyone I had missed so dearly, especially Jayden and our substances.

We got off of the exit that my father's house was next to, and I noticed not much had changed. The city was identical. All the same families surrounded us, and the middle-class, mediocre town was the spitting image of what I had left. When we pulled up the driveway, my dad's two dogs were barking their heads off, my stepmother gave me her condescending hello, and foremost I knew there was no way I could possibly stay at my father's house – just like it was in high school. I immediately noticed the new furniture, fixtures, and adjustments when I walked into the house. I noticed my room had changed, or, better yet, been completely eliminated. My room was no longer a room, but instead was a storage unit for my father and stepmom's excess eBay items. They must have gotten heavy into personal E-commerce, and saw my room as an opportunity for more inventory. This was perfectly fine with me, since I wouldn't have to make an excuse to bail on my father when I wanted to be under the influence at Jayden's. It was already assumed that I would be residing in Jayden's detached apartment until we departed for Radford. This was assumed by both my family and his.

After a couple hours of playing catch-up with my father, discussing business, work, school, and other father/son topics, I decided to text Jayden to see what he was up to. When I contacted Jayden, we proceeded to make arrangements for staying at the apartment. Jayden told me to hurry up and get over there to start celebrating. As soon as I got there, we started talking about the wild days of junior and senior year. The reminiscing must have engaged ideas to bring the memories of the past back to memories in the making. We all had a look of happiness thinking about these times. These spawned ideas in all of us to make them happen once again. With that said, Braden suggested we do some ecstasy and shrooms to celebrate the reunion.

Jayden and I looked at each other and knew exactly what that look meant – hell yeah! We relentlessly went through our cell phones until we found someone with beautiful gold-cap mushrooms. Ironically, they were from the same dealer we'd had in high school. He was extremely surprised to hear from me, but regardless was down for the sale as always. We bought a half ounce, and we decided we would split the shrooms in three ways. We put the shrooms in Fruit Roll-Ups to mask the dreadful taste and ate them whole. We all participated in the ridiculous theories that an individual can only think about while under such a heavy substance, all regarding time, space, and existence.

This trip was strange to me for a couple reasons. Firstly, the cartoon animation of myself did not appear the entire night. Secondly, to accompany the first fact, I hated that my animated figure wasn't there while I was tripping. It was almost as if I was subconsciously looking for him the entire night. The animated figure had become a routinized part of my trips. Despite those strange aspects of this trip, it was one of fun, amusement, and reminiscence. We were dancing, laughing, and sincerely enjoying the time of rejoicing in one another's company. After our festivities, Braden fell asleep and Jayden and I talked about how we would be attending the same university in just one short week. Our late night/early morning conversations gradually led to the dreadful feeling of sobriety. This made me wonder if I was rejoicing my old life, or if I was rejoicing the fact that I once again could do substances with no limitation.

That next week, I was on the phone more than a telemarketer, making relentless attempts to get in contact with several of Radford's departments, including the admission office, financial aid, and residential life. It was a consistent daily mixture of working on getting everything squared away regarding Radford during the day, and of course partying at night. I finally had gotten through to admissions. This resulted in them sending over all the information and documentation necessary to register for Quest (which was their freshman seminar), as well as the access I needed to register for classes. Financial aid also got back to me with good news – my tuition had cleared thanks to Federal Student Loans (FAFSA). Everything was coming together!

With only a few days left, there was one department that had not gotten back to me: residential life. Residential life is in charge of on-campus housing options. I was entering in the spring semester. With that said, it was already extremely difficult to find an open dormitory, and it was getting harder as time passed. When the department finally did contact me, the news was not as fortunate as what I'd received from the other departments. In layman's terms, I was in a "SOL" situation. I was accepted by admissions, had paid my tuition by financial aid, but was screwed in regards to housing while I was attending the university. I knew I needed to formulate a plan B. I decided to look into off-campus housing close enough to campus where a car would not be needed, but not so close that it was owned by Radford University.

If you remember, I'd sold my vehicle along with other belongings to assist me financially in getting back to Virginia, enrolling in the university, minimizing student loans, and of course to fulfill my substance desires. I needed to find a place now that was not considered on-campus housing, but close enough where bus or foot transportation was possible. As options and resources given by the university seemed they were coming to a close, I decided to take the desperate measure of going through classified ads on Craigslist. I saw an array of ads under "rooms for rent," although with distance and limited income being a factor many of those options were eliminated, leaving only about two or three realistic options.

After calling the two or three realistic options, the best one seemed to be rooming with an individual named Tammy. Tammy lived in a two-bedroom house and her roommate needed to move out. She said that he'd failed out of college, and that was all I knew about the house. The house looked as if it were falling apart online, but at a bit over three hundred dollars per month and three blocks away from the school I assured myself the benefits outweighed the risk. It was the only option I had to lock in immediately, although I was nervous about the fact that I could not see the house until it was time for school to start. I needed to make a decision, and knowing the house was ready immediately, was cheap, and no deposit was necessary made it seem to be the most logical decision at the time. I figured if this was the final commitment to enrolling at Radford University I would do it!

The last day in my high-school town was filled with mixed emotions. I was ecstatic to start a new life with my best friend, but I was upset I only got to see the rest of the crew for only one short week. Stephanie, Braden, Ricky, Jayden, and I certainly lived it up in that short week. We met up nearly every night, drinking, smoking, and doing a variety of drugs until the crack of dawn. Once this amazing week came to a close, I once again found myself giving the rounds of goodbyes and packing my belongings to head up to college.

I had to use a significant amount of discretion while packing due to the fact that I only had one carload of space to fill in my father's 2001 Hyundai Santa Fe. I was essentially starting from scratch all over again, but this time I felt a lot more comfortable knowing I was not going to have the fear of being sober. It seems like an irrational fear, but to an addict it is very serious, real, and accompanied by a large amount of anxiety. The lack of anxiety made it extremely easy to formulate the best plan of action to execute.

The game plan was to pack my father's car the Saturday morning that I was giving my goodbyes, but depart for Radford in Jayden's vehicle. Mr. Powers, still thinking Jayden and I were innocent buddies, was going to drop us off in Radford that Saturday to ensure that Jayden could show me the campus and introduce me to people the day before Quest (new-student orientation), which was on that Sunday. Mr. Powers and my father believed this would help me to obtain a better understanding of the university and the environment. To us, this meant a night before things needed to be done, meaning we could do our poison of choice and have a great first night!

The second step of the plan was for my dad to drive up Sunday after a business meeting to help me finalize the student loans he was cosigning on. He would meet me at the residence before Quest to ensure everything was going smoothly. We were both there to prioritize what needed to be accomplished in order to be positive that school was squared away for that Monday. Anyone dealing with, or who has dealt with, enrolling in higher education can conclude that there are many aspects that must work in your favor to ensure you will be admitted, registered, and enrolled.

The first step in executing what we had been working on went just as planned. Saturday morning Jayden, Mr. Powers, and I prepared for our long drive to Radford University. We were talking about the college experience for nearly six hours straight, something I had never experienced for myself. Mr. Powers was telling us all about his substance, sexual, and "academic" adventures, thinking we were just two innocent kids who had never experienced any of it. The stories made me extremely anxious to experience that life at a higher magnitude than high school, and it wouldn't be long before I did.

After the extremely long drive, Mr. Powers dropped us off in front of Jayden's dorm, where Jayden and I split paths for the time being. One of the first things I did was establish a PO box, and I told my dad I wanted one so he could send packages through the post office regardless of where I resided. The reality was that I needed it for my "goodbye" card from Los Angeles, and that was its sole purpose. Before I met with Jayden, I called Milley to tell her the necessary information, and she confirmed it was being sent. I wasn't ready to tell anyone about this venture, but I was not going to back out.

After the phone call, I met Jayden at his dorm. I met his roommate Donald and his suitemate Gunter. They were both extremely welcoming, especially Gunter. In fact, his first welcoming words were, "What's up, man, you want a shot of Everclear?" I agreed with absolutely no hesitation. I thought to myself, "I am in heaven..." It hadn't even been twenty minutes that I was at the university, it was three o'clock in the afternoon, and the atmosphere was lining up perfectly with what I wanted from a college experience. We were all drinking as they were telling me all the wild stories from fall semester, giving me a taste of what my semester was going to be like. By five o'clock, I'd forgotten about all the responsibilities I needed to embrace the following day, such as Quest, registering for classes, financial aid, and my housing situation.

I needed to start this long adventure at 8:00 a.m., but I was drunk so none of those responsibilities mattered to me at that time. My first night in Radford was amazing, and that was all that mattered. My first night lived up to the hype to say the least. After drinking in the dorms for nearly four hours, we went party-hopping in the peak hours of the night. I told the group that Jayden had introduced me to repeatedly that it was the best night of my life. They replied with a smile, as if it was *deja vu* to their night before Quest the previous semester. Essentially, their first night at the university (known as "Freshman Friday").

The parties were outrageous, almost like something you would imagine at a modern-day *Animal House*. Cocaine, MDMA, marijuana, and mass amounts of alcohol were being offered everywhere we turned, and I sure as hell accepted those offers. Jayden, Gunter, a couple girls, and I headed back to the dormitory about a half a mile away from where we living up our night. My night ended with projectile vomiting in the hallway of the residential hall as Jayden was trying to keep me away from security. He successfully got me into his dorm and onto the tile floor with no security or trouble involved. I puked in the suite's bathroom while everyone was joking around saying things like "Turn up or transfer" all in good fun. I fell asleep with a huge smile on my face as the room spun, and Jayden set the alarm for me that would give me a rude awakening at 7:30 a.m. to get ready for Quest, my new-student orientation.

After a deep, almost deathly, sleep, I remained unconscious while the blaring alarm was continually going off. I finally jerked myself off the floor at 8:15 a.m., realizing I was late to the Quest orientation. I sprang up off of the floor and threw some water on my face to try and sober up from the night before. I had only gotten a couple hours of sleep, and that surely was not enough sleep for my brain to recover. With the same clothes I'd been wearing the previous night, a horrendous hairdo, and some puke on the side of my mouth, I ran out the dormitory toward the student resource center as fast as I possibly could. My head was pounding, I was irritated, my surroundings were spinning, and my addicted mind did not regret it one bit. The only thing I regretted slightly was the fact that my father was going to see me in the state I was in, and there was no way he was going to be at ease with that. My first night there was amazing, but my first morning was a wreck.

My father saw me and looked concerned, but of course I justified myself by assuring him I was just up late "catching up" with Jayden. I continued by stating this resulted in me almost staying up all night. My father still believed me, with a hesitant look of acceptance on his face. In his head I was still the same innocent little boy who preached sobriety. He didn't know whether to believe that I was just "hanging out." He was offish and hesitant while proceeding to take care of my enrollment, but continued to stay naïve about my substance abuse. I needed to make sure my father was okay when he left and not too concerned; believe it or not, that was very important to me. This was necessary to me because I did not want him to know I was doing the substances, and secondly I dreaded the thought of him blaming himself – which he always had a habit of doing. Regardless of my reasoning, I attempted to stay alert and focused around my father to minimize his suspicions about what we were up to the night before.

I was trying my absolute hardest to stay conscious during the seminar, but I failed at that miserably. I was fading in and out of consciousness from the second I sat down, and I had fallen asleep moments after the seminar had started. I missed the entire first portion of Quest, where they explained how meal plans, student activities, enrollment, financial aid, and an array of other departments operated on campus. The second portion of Quest was designated for touring the campus, which if it weren't for a peer I would have missed as well, having almost slept through it.

When a fellow Quest participant shook my shoulder and said, "You have too much fun last night, bro?" I sprang up. He informed me we were all leaving to tour the campus. I was in misery touring the campus, and it didn't help that it was absolutely freezing outside… I was woozy, irritated, and just wanted to sleep as we were walking through what would soon be my sanctuary for the next four years. I would break from the group almost every time I saw a bathroom to hack my brains out. As I was living in my own misery touring the campus, my father was finalizing the process of my student loans. When my father and I met again around 3:00 p.m., we had the admissions and financial aid squared away, leaving one more mission, finalizing the off-campus housing.

We left with a packet filled with all the documentation to prove that I was eligible to start my education at Radford University. We got it in just in time; classes started on that following day. We hopped in the car and drove to Tammy's to finalize the lease. She walked out looking similar to me when I woke up. Her hairdo was as rough as mine, she came out with a cut-up Led Zeppelin shirt on, and she looked as if she had woken up no more than thirty minutes prior to showing us the house.

She looked like a true modern millennial hippie. I knew she was a typical college partier, and despite the run-down house, at least I knew my roommate and I would get along instantly. When my father and I walked into the house, he looked extremely concerned about the living conditions. It was not so much the physical structure of the house, but the items in the household that we could only assume were owned by Tammy. His overwhelming look of concern correlated perfectly to my thoughts of excitement. Essentially, all the reasons he was concerned were all the identical reasons I had to be excited. It looked as if Philip's layout in his small Los Angeles room had spread throughout an entire house here at Radford University. The top of the cabinet was covered in liquor bottles, the walls were blanketed by tapestries, and there were four or five pieces of hand-blown glass paraphernalia in a corner in the living room. As we walked in, Tammy subtly whispered in my ear, "Sorry, I didn't know your father was going to come." I then gave a genuine smile and laughed, insinuating that we had the same interests.

My father and I walked back outside to talk about whether we were willing to go through with this house and unload my stuff from the back of my father's car. I didn't have furniture since I couldn't fit anything else in the car besides my microphone, some clothes, memorabilia, and other materials that were essential. My father looked nervous and took a deep breath, and I knew exactly what he was going to say before he even finished his drawn-out sigh of nervousness. My father wanted to talk me out of living in that house due to the fact that it reeked of marijuana, contained an array of illegal items, and looked as if it were a "flophouse" in Compton. All of the reasons that he felt were detrimental to my well-being (and he was right) were the exact reasons I wanted to convince him that this was a good place, but obviously I couldn't say that.

With an addict's deception skills, I knew it would not be all too difficult to get what I wanted, which of course was to reside at that house. My deceptive mind told me I needed to successfully convince my father that this was the best option due to the facts that several college students were going to have similar items in the household, I wouldn't be in the house much, when I was in the residence I would be in my room, and I would be paying the rent, and this was the cheapest place.

After contemplation my father hesitantly agreed with me, and we decided to proceed with signing the lease. When we asked Tammy about the lease, or even the whereabouts of the landlord, she took a pause as if her brain shut off. She informed us that I could move in, but the landlord was not around. She continued by relaying the information from the landlord that he would be around this week, and I could sign the lease within the next couple days. It definitely was not traditional, but nonetheless we started moving the little I had into the house.

We opened the door to the almost-empty room, where the ex-roommate was throwing the last of his belongings into a box. As he was walking out the door, my father noticed a bed and a dresser were still in the room. After my dad told me that I asked him what he was going to do with the two items and if he was interested in selling them for forty bucks. Without any hesitation, he agreed! "Hell yeah, man, I didn't know what I was going to do with them anyway. That works!" he said with relief. Everything was all set. I was enrolled, I was registered for classes, those classes were paid for, and I had a room that I could call my own – something I hadn't had in almost two years.

After everything was settled in, I walked my father outside to say my goodbyes, and he still had an overwhelming look of concern. I assured him it would be okay, and that I was bettering myself in regards to education and self-growth. He gave me a nod of approval, one last hug, and got into his vehicle not knowing I was making the biggest mistake of my life. As soon as my father left I called Jayden over and he was at my house within minutes to check out the new setup. We smoked our welcoming bowl within minutes of him being here and instantly knew this was going to be the new hangout spot. We found out that my new roommate was a drug dealer, had no worries about us using her paraphernalia, and that we could do drugs there in the open anytime of any day!

Jayden and I sat back on the couch and thought about how awesome this was going to be. The next four years living in paradise. Jayden had the resources for the fun dormitory experience, and I had the house where we could do whatever we wanted whenever we wanted. As we were discussing the new setup, the opportunity for partying, and the great new hangout spot, Jayden sprang out of his chair and said, "Dude, your birthday party needs to be here!!"

My birthday is January 25th, and fell on the very first Friday that we were back at school. After Jayden instilled this idea in my head, I knew that we had to do something epic for my first birthday at Radford. I knew I wanted an enormous crowd of people, and I knew I wanted Braden and Stephanie there to celebrate with us. As Jayden and I were planning out the specifics of throwing this raging party and gathering all the details, the crew from high school worked on getting to Radford. Sure enough, the plan was strategized to be executed perfectly.

Braden agreed to drive up to Radford and make a pit-stop at Kingsdale to pick up Stephanie. This contribution from Braden made it possible for my friends to come out for my birthday bash! I was ecstatic – my three favorite people from high school were going to be at my party, although I was nervous about the fact that most of Jayden's colleagues had failed out their first semester at Radford University. This made me nervous because I had not met more than ten or fifteen people, and I wanted that party to be the talk of the campus.

Although several of Jayden's colleagues had failed out, he was able to introduce me to one girl who went by the name of Rachel, and she seemed to know the whole campus. More specifically, she seemed to know a lot of people with the same interests as Jayden and I. Rachel had dark-red hair, faintly placed freckles and piercings on her face, and tattoos that blanketed her body. The first night we met I was in "lust." She had a rebellious lifestyle similar to mine, with stories about deviance, drugs, and chaos. I fell in love with her rebellious lifestyle. Jayden claimed that she was the female version of me, and I completely saw where he drew that conclusion from.

Rachel, Jayden, some other new connections, and I sat around my living room doing MDMA a couple days before my party was set to take place. We were having the time of our life doing absolutely nothing. We were listening to music that brought on relaxing vibes, smoking the best marijuana we could find in the small town of

Radford, and sharing the hysterical stories of Jayden and me in our high school days. These rebellious stories seemed to grasp Rachel's attention, resulting in a flirty "hard-to-get" type of relationship between the two of us. We had no idea what the feelings were, but we knew that we both felt some way about the other.

The exchange of stories of our chaotic pasts strengthened this unexplainable bond that was blossoming between Rachel and me. A new duo in crime seemed to be forming between the two of us. It got to the point that we were the only two that were sharing our insane stories while the rest of the group listened in disbelief. Jayden saw it too, and it looked as if he was hesitating to tell me something about the situation we all saw taking place, a dangerous bond forming. Although I could tell he had an urge to tell me something, he just smiled at me and we continued with our euphoric night. When I felt the uncomfortable vibes Jayden's body language was giving off, I decided to steer the conversation back to planning the party. I simply stated, "Let's get back to the party, we have a lot of planning to do." We got back on the topic of the party, and we all sat around the coffee table exchanging our thoughts about the party that was going to be the real-life *Project X,* especially with the LSD that was bound to arrive.

After Rachel and Jayden assured me that they knew enough people to cover the house in partiers, booze, and drugs, I felt a lot better about the situation, and decided I would continue with my pleasant reminiscing. Rachel and I continued sharing stories, and came to the conclusion that we were the same out-of-control type of person. We loved that fact, and that sole fact was the base of a wild relationship that was starting to build at a fast rate. Whether it was the drugs or the company that I was with, I had such an awesome time hanging out in my new house with this new group of people, especially this girl Rachel. The first night we met, I could not stop looking at her. Daydreaming, as if she were the girl I was looking for, but something held me back.

The feeling that was hindering me from making any moves on her was a discussion Stephanie and I'd had before I left my visit in

Ridge Run. We had talked about maybe giving us a shot as something more significant than a friendship, an actual intimate relationship. Once I got back to Ridge Run, Stephanie seemed to be the norm, and whether it was real or not, I felt a sense of love when I was in her presence. One night during winter break we were all together in Ridge Run, all under the influence of ecstasy. Stephanie and I found ourselves in one of Jayden's rooms in the apartment. We were both absolutely wasted, and that had resulted in a sexual encounter in Jayden's apartment that had sparked strong feelings toward one another.

I did feel some type of lustful "love" for Rachel, but I knew Stephanie was undoubtedly a better companion for my wellbeing. She was in school while Rachel had failed out, Stephanie was a marijuana smoker while Rachel was a full-blown drug junkie, Stephanie had a sole focus on me while Rachel was sleeping around with several guys, and Stephanie was a woman with self-respect while Rachel lacked it completely. I had enough reality at the time to realize those differences, and I figured Rachel and I were better off as friends. There was nothing to tell Rachel at the time, because no intimacy was attempted by either her or myself. Rachel and I knew that feelings were there, but we also knew that neither of us was going to make a move on the other.

That Friday night was finally here, the night of the wild party. Jayden, Stephanie, and another girl named Katlyn knocked on the door to my residence that was falling to the ground. I stumbled to the door and opened it, already heavily intoxicated at 4:00 p.m. Stephanie gave me an enormous hug and a peck on the lips, wishing me a happy birthday. Jayden got a peck on the lips as well from Katlyn. The two were best friends and partners in crime, with one of their crimes being the fact that they were dating us two buffoons. Katlyn and I were not all that close, although if you were close to Jayden you were also held dear to me. After those two encounters with our significant others Braden just laughed and stated, "That is so freaking weird, all of you are my friends…"

I gave my good friends a tour of the house and we smoked a welcoming bowl around the coffee table. As we were catching up, Rachel and the rest of my new connections walked through the door. Rachel was full of life, but within seconds that extroverted personality went down the drain. Stephanie was sitting on my lap when Rachel gave her an awkward look, and Stephanie gave her a mutual facial expression in return. Why did Rachel look so surprised? This was extremely awkward for me as well, but knowing I had done nothing wrong made me feel good about myself.

The morals and values that were instilled in me since my childhood, even though the temptation was there, prevailed at this point in time. I may have been an addict at the time, but I had never been a cheater. I had no intention of starting now regardless of how incredibly strong the temptation was. They met with a fake smile and Rachel said the classic "It's nice to meet you," although I knew it was with a condescending nature. Rachel was a little too friendly with me, which made Stephanie a bit uneasy. But I assured Steph that she was just being a little possessive of me.

Rachel had brought some friends with her that Jayden and I had been building relationships with. These friends were not the type of people my old friends would think we would actually become acquainted with. Jayden and I knew they felt a bit uncomfortable. We pulled them to the side and let them know these were not our best friends, rather just the people that were going to make the party possible. We continued by assuring them they didn't have to be best friends, but it was important that we all got along so we could have an awesome party. We fabricated their personalities, making them seem like awesome people. In reality, they were far from friends and we barely knew them, but we did know that they were our resources for booze and drugs. We reunited with the group that was making my friends uncomfortable when Rachel's friend Jake introduced himself to my high-school gang.

Jake was also a mutual friend of Tammy's. They weren't friends necessarily, but more like "family" in the sense that he'd known her since childhood. Braden, Stephanie, and Katlyn seemed extremely uncomfortable around him due to his strung-out look and abnormal comments. He was socially awkward and his speech was slow and slurred. Jake told us that with Tammy's, Rachel's, and his assistance they could set up an amazing party. He went in depth about past celebrations they'd thrown last year with an array of wild stories that captured our attention. He continued to make conversation, perhaps providing too much information. He threw his "good friend" Tammy into the conversation, essentially throwing her under the bus and giving us an in-depth insight into who she truly was.

She was a girlfriend to a man serving five years for armed robbery, a thief herself, and a huge pill popper. This didn't surprise me, but I wasn't expecting someone to actually confirm the assumptions I had about her. Jake admitted to pill usage as well, but he claimed he was a good person and truly "wanted" sobriety. He proceeded to put himself on a pedestal, and he wanted to forewarn me about Tammy's tendencies before I was caught by surprise. He claimed that she would accuse her old roommate of stealing her drugs when in reality she took them and forgot. He said this was a direct cause of his moving out, which was why I had acquired the room in the first place. The "failing out" was a lie made up by Tammy.

Lastly, he told me she received sketchy packages in the mail that could make me feel uncomfortable. I didn't say anything, but I was pondering where my sketchy package in the mail was. I was smart enough to send it to a PO box, but it had been almost two weeks. Anyway, I looked at Rachel for her to confirm what he was saying, since I had no idea who this guy was, or how reliable that information was. Unfortunately, Rachel did not have anything further to add due to the fact that she had only started hanging out at Tammy's after she learned Jayden and I spent most of our day there. Jayden and I concluded that we were going to have to find out for ourselves, because Jake was obviously not the most credible source.

We decided to brush it off, and start setting up the party...and the same thought kept popping up in my head: whatever happened to the LSD? I'd told Milley the PO box address well over a week ago. I decided I needed to call her. After countless times of reaching her voicemail, I finally accepted the fact that her phone was disconnected, and so was her boyfriend's. This would make anyone realize they needed to settle down and keep their nose clean for a while, but not an addict. The LSD never arrived at the destination, which would scare the average person. To this day, I'm not positive how the situation played out, but this still was not enough for me to stop. In an addict's mind, this seems like pure misfortune that could never happen to them. Instead of lying low for their safety and staying away from illegal activity, they typically ignore the situation at hand. Sure, I was worried for my friends, but the addict in me thought, "How will me quitting help their situation at all?"

With that said, I started my night by doing MDMA with an incredibly extroverted guy named Colton that Rachel and Jayden introduced me to. Colton was a big hilarious Puerto Rican who had me laughing all night, both from his MDMA and comical jokes. He was good friends with both Jayden and Rachel, and was another connection I was extremely fortunate to make. He was the life of the party, and he usually brought over ten girls with him to the parties he attended. I knew Colton and I were going to become extremely close due to the similarities in our personalities and interests. He had also brought his roommate, Alex. Alex was a transfer from VMI. He was an admirable military man who was studying to be a chemist. Being in the National Guard made it impossible to be into the drug scene, but he was not judgmental due to the fact that he was a BIG drinker. He reminded me of myself in the sense that he enjoyed getting hammered and being destructive. He was a wild military man who treated Radford's small town as his own personal demolishing zone.

As he was telling me his stories, I informed him he had just found a partner in crime. Stephanie laughed and assured him that was more than a true statement. I hung out with these two goons, Jayden, Braden, Stephanie, and Katlyn the majority of the night, trying to avoid Rachel and any conflict associated with her. Rachel was not keeping me out of sight. In fact, I caught her staring from afar all night, flirting with all of my friends, attempting to grasp my attention. Unfortunately, she was capturing my jealousy. The party was lively and extremely diverse in regards to the substances, music preferences, and the types of people that it consisted of – druggies, college students, sketchballs, dean's list students, and everything in between. We played everything from reggae to dirty-south rap. There were hallucinogens, uppers, downers, alcohol, marijuana, stimulants, opiates, and any other drug you could imagine somewhere in the house

Everyone was having an amazing time, even Tammy. I had a bad feeling that was going to rapidly change once I noticed Tammy rummaging through the kitchen drawers. From that moment, I knew Jake was not fabricating. My gut told me that she was going to raise hell momentarily. My gut prevailed, and that is exactly what happened within five minutes. She stormed into the living room where everyone was dancing, shut down the party in a psychotic manner, and demanded everyone leave the house immediately, except for Jayden and, of course, myself. She silenced the music, kicked everyone out, and slammed the door behind them. Colton and Alex were walking out with the crowd as fast as possible, but before they had reached the door, they let me know I could crash there if things got out of control. Jake trailed behind the crowd as he whispered to me, "I told you, bro." Rachel followed directly behind Jake, and walked out the door, giving me her seductive look.

After everyone had left the residence, we sat there as if we were being held hostage. Due to what Jake had told us earlier, I knew exactly what was going to happen. Sure enough, Tammy started accusing Jayden and me of stealing her Xanax, and we both had seen it coming a mile away. At first, we were not sure what to do. We were in complete shock in this situation. After about forty minutes of interrogation, I told her that the argument was going to go nowhere due to the fact that I truly had no idea where her pills were. She continued yelling, and I knew I had no other option except to fight fire with fire. I needed to fight or flight, and my choice was evident. She accused Jayden and me because we were so intoxicated, although our polysubstance binge was provided by Colton's connections. I finally told her to go f*ck herself, that she was a junky and probably had taken the pills and forgotten. She started bawling, her jaw dropped, and she went silent. I continued by giving her the bird, feeling no remorse, and I walked out of the residence filled with anger.

My furious rage brought me and my friends to accept our new acquaintance's offer of staying at his residence. Colton completely went through with his offer and didn't seem surprised to see us there within minutes after he left the party. Jayden jokingly said, "Yeah, Brad has a little temper when it comes to being yelled at like that." Tammy learned very quickly that I was not going to put up with that, and changes were going to be made if she wanted me as a roommate. Rachel was also at Colton's, which spawned several issues in itself. She seemed sexually attracted to my temper that had come out that night, and Stephanie saw it instantly.

Stephanie pulled me to the side to go on a "walk." Anyone can infer when a girlfriend wants to go on a walk at 1:00 a.m., something is wrong. My prediction was proven to be correct. With that being said, she wanted to warn me how she saw the look in Rachel's eyes when she gazed at me. She asked me if I noticed it, how I felt about it, and what I was going to do about it. I felt an argument inevitably happening due to the nature of what accompanies talking about another girl with your girlfriend. The fact that tensions were already through the roof from what happened at Tammy's didn't help either. I took a deep breath before I answered her array of question and answered by calmly explaining to Stephanie that I had been in enough arguments for one day…especially my birthday. Stephanie, being the good girlfriend that she was, decided to be the bigger person and suggested that we go back to Colton's and try to enjoy the rest of the night with one another.

Colton and Alex lived with each other in an apartment complex that was literally right next door to my run-down residence. I walked into the two-bedroom apartment for the very first time, and Colton was extremely welcoming. I let him know what had happened after Tammy flipped out. He jokingly said, "Maybe you signed a lease a little too early." I kept silent, hoping he would elaborate on what he meant.

He continued by telling me that a guy had just moved out of the living room. His deal was pretty simple and straightforward – two hundred bucks flat. Since he was staying in the living room, with not as much privacy, he had no financial obligations to internet, utilities, cable, etc. This seemed pretty logical to me, and I wished I had met Colton a couple days prior to moving into Tammy's. It was an amazing deal that he only could have put on the table a week ago. I was obsessed about how awesome this deal was for days on end while we were hanging out! While I was pondering that thought I realized I hadn't signed the lease! I had no legal obligation to stay in that house.

If you recall, the landlord was going to meet me before rent was due to finish the signing, but that would be cruel to leave Tammy in the dust, despite her intoxicated outrage. Furthermore, it would be wrong to live for free while I was there and then leave days before rent was due. Even though this was morally wrong, I would save almost a couple hundred dollars a month on rent, roughly seventy-five dollars on utilities, and an additional forty-five dollars a month on internet. I was completely torn... This was an amazing financial opportunity, but my moral values hindered this chance to capitalize on this opportunity. I may have been an addict, but I still had morals – kind of. With that said, I could not morally accept Colton's offer. I did, however, consistently think about how he really turned the night around for all of us, and it would be amazing to have a roommate like that.

Stephanie and I woke up cuddling on Colton's couch, Jayden found himself on the floor right near the laundry room next to Katlyn, Braden had gone to a dorm with a girl he met at the party, and Rachel had fallen asleep in Colton's bed – probably another attempt to capture my jealousy. We woke up and went to go find Braden. Once we found Braden in a dorm close to Jayden's, we all went to go enjoy a meal at the campus student buffet. After an enjoyable meal I figured I might as well go back to the house and have the conversation with Tammy that everybody was dreading to witness.

I am trying to keep this book as PG as possible, but to say the least, I had said awful degrading things to Tammy that I knew had to be discussed. I felt awful because of the things I said, but I also believed that it was necessary to shut down her intoxicated rage. After dealing with my drunk stepfather, I had promised myself I would never let someone degrade me in an intoxicated outburst like that ever again. With that said, I realized she was my roommate and we were going to have to clear the air if there was any chance of improving our relationship. We finished our meal at the cafeteria and dragged our feet toward my house.

We walked up the sagging steps, and I walked alone through the door while my friends waited in the front yard. I was instantly overwhelmed with anger from the previous night. Tammy was in the living room with a distraught look. She asked where my "backup" was, implying the friends who came to visit. I informed her my friends were waiting outside. She put her head into her hands, and surprisingly, her first words were "I'm sorry."

My initial reaction was to accept the apology, and I took a deep breath. While I was in middle of the drawn-out breath, my mind flashed back to the night before. After that flashback occurred I had a change in attitude, and it was far from accepting the apology I received. Her apology gave me an advantage in the argument, and my corrupted mind told me to take advantage of it. I started by telling her to stay away from me. I proceeded to tell her I knew the reasons why her roommate moved out, and I made it clear I wasn't going to be bullied out of the house by a raging drug junkie. I let her know she could bet her bottom dollar next time something like that happened, she would be the one leaving the residence in the backseat of a cop car to visit her boyfriend.

She was in shock to find how much I already knew about her. As she started crying, I continued by asking rhetorical questions such as: Are you the landlord? Are you my mother? Are you the property manager? My voice started to escalate in volume as her eyes were suctioned to the ground. She was unsure how to respond. There was a moment of silence. I wrapped my rant up by stating, "This is our house, not yours. The faster you realize that, the better off everyone will be." I made it clear there were going to be no more demands, and if she raised hell and embarrassed me like she had, she would see a whole new side to me.

After that conversation, she didn't come out of her room much. She kept her distance due to the fact that if she attempted to be friendly, I would shut her down with no hesitation. Everyone noticed that the dominant one in the house had changed, all as a result of the night of my birthday party. Jake couldn't believe she'd backed down to me so easily. He told me no one had ever gotten to Tammy so severely, not even him, who had been her friend for over a decade. He said people had always been afraid to give her a reality slap due to the fact that they knew her boyfriend and his insanely violent past.

Everyone that knew her tendencies gained a lot respect for me. It wasn't what I had expected, but the party itself and the aftermath became the talk of the town. I was known as the person who gave Tammy a reality slap and put an end to her egotistic rage. Furthermore, I was the kid from L.A. who had spunk, the new kid that didn't take anything from anyone, and the wild best friend that Jayden had bragged about months before I had even stepped foot on Radford's campus. The narcotics and respect that blanketed my real personality started to give me an out-of-control ego that started to form the real, and new, me...the same exact ego I was supposedly "fighting" against. Before I knew it, I was the one who had the drug-addict attitude, the narcissistic mindset, and the outlook no one could change, and the worst part was everyone respected it in my falsified reality.

Even though my legitimate issues regarding living in a house with Tammy were resolved, it was getting harder to decline Colton's offer, which could be the subconscious reason I did not want to let go of the tension between us. First off, it was so much cheaper. Secondly, I was becoming good friends with Alex and Colton. Lastly, I sincerely hated Tammy. I needed to make the move, but I felt as if I was stuck regardless of the fact that the landlord still had not presented any legal documentation. It was early February, and I was patiently waiting for my landlord to visit the residence to meet him and sign the lease. I was living in the house, off the books, for nearly three weeks. The first week of February was coming to a close and the landlord called me to inform me I could pay February's rent the second week of February when he came to the premises.

He was not aware that I was already paying bills, receiving mail, and everything else that accompanies a new residence. I told him I would not be doing anything but moving my stuff in until the lease was finalized. With that said, I requested he mail me a copy of the lease to hurry up the process. I made it seem as if I was waiting to "officially" move in until I had signed and processed all of the legalities. He agreed that it would be better for him to send the lease via USPS. Firstly, he lived 150 miles away and if he utilized USPS he would not have to make the physical trip to Radford. Secondly, he felt bad about the fact I was "waiting" to "officially" move in.

A couple days after we had that call, I was constantly checking the mail for the lease. I opened the taped-together mailbox and there was a package. The package was not for me or Tammy. In fact, it wasn't addressed to anyone I'd even heard of. I picked up the extremely light package to see it had our address on it, but it was for someone named Jose. I took it into my room, confused about what to do with the package. It sat in the corner for the day. I wanted to make sure it was returned to the sender. I figured I would just call USPS when I got back from class. When I got back from my 3:00 class, Colton was hanging out in my room waiting for me. The first question he asked me was in regards to the suspicious box in the corner of my room.

He firmly believed it was a box that contained drugs. He reminded me about what Jake said about Tammy, and he continued by claiming he knew a sketchy package when he saw one. I gave him an ambiguous laugh. I was unsure if he was serious. I stared at the box for a couple seconds and brushed it off as if he said it in a comical manner. As soon as we changed the topic, I heard a timid knock on my door. When I asked who it was Tammy answered. I unlocked the door and Tammy walked in. I heard her soft voice ask, "You didn't see a package in the mailbox, did you?" Colton and I looked at one another, and I instantly claimed that I hadn't seen anything.

As soon as I shut my door, Colton looked at me, suggesting he was right about the package. I bolted to the corner of my room to open the box. There was a tub of Planters peanuts and a banana. I looked at Colton with a confused expression. He made direct eye contact and said, "Dude, trust me, open it." At first glance, I figured they were peanuts, but why would someone send peanuts and a banana? I opened the Planters tub and it was pills, a lot of pills. There must have been nearly a thousand Xanax pills in this tub. My heart dropped, and I thought of three options: I can simply give it to Tammy and explain I didn't know it was hers due to the unknown name, I could steal them and make 100% profit on the endeavor, or I could use this as blackmail and ultimately an escape from her house.

I needed something like this to diminish the lease. I desperately needed leverage so she wouldn't tell the landlord I had lived there three weeks in order to move out with no legal conflict. I figured ducking out days before rent was due could have definitely gotten me in legal trouble, but now I had something that could get her years in prison. I told Colton the three outcomes that could result from these pills. He laughed and jokingly said, "New roomies." That was exactly what was going on in my head, and that was the choice I was set on. At this point I was not a thief, and I definitely was not going to help out such a horrible person.

I hid the box in my closet, locked my door, and we went to go make sure it was okay with Alex to have a second roommate. Alex was excited and agreed to the proposition without hesitation. He knew that it was going to be the awesome college trio of partying and chaos that all three of us wanted. We all got along so well, and I wanted the journey to start immediately. With that said, we decided to get started right then and there. When we got back to my house I took a deep breath, grabbed the package, and walked out with my chest out to start the nerve-racking conversation.

Tammy and Jake were sitting on the couch when I advised Jake he might want to leave for a minute. He smiled at me, knowing that I was probably going to put Tammy in her place once again. It made him happy knowing someone was not afraid of her convict lover. When he saw the package in my hand, his eyes grew enormously and he sprang off the couch. He knew what it was. Before Jake even had a foot out of the front door, Tammy took a deep breath to yell at me. She screamed about half of my name when I told her to shut her mouth. She did immediately with a face full of rage. She bit her tongue as I threw the pills onto the coffee table, looked her dead in the eye, and started to explain the fact that she only had two options. I took a deep breath and explained the two scenarios she had to choose from, and it was completely up to her.

"Tammy, you have two options. Put it this way: one of two phone calls will be made." I started giving the more predictable outcome she would choose of her two scenarios, although she thought the first option was the irrational one. She was in for a rude awakening, because I knew I needed a scot-free way out of that hellion's household. "Tammy, here is option A. All of my belongings are going to be out of the house by the time you get back from class, meaning I will not be signing the lease that the landlord sent here the other day."

Her jaw dropped in disbelief of how strong I was coming off. I continued, "I am sure we both realize he is going to call me once he realizes no lease is being signed and returned…but he is not going to get an answer from me. More than likely, he is going to call you to see what is going on. You are going to tell him I never moved in or came to the premises, and I must no longer have interest in signing the lease." She instantly refused. Still in disbelief, she exclaimed I was out of my mind and she was not going to be stuck paying the bills on her own the entire year.

She continued by giving me a sob story of how hard it was to find a roommate, and I was her one shot of not being financially screwed during the school year. She continued by explaining how her mom was paying her bills, and she really did not want to explain how another roommate left her. I cut her off to assure her that none of that was relevant to the situation at hand. She desperately apologized again and sighed, "So what is my second option? Stop doing drugs, are you my dad now?"

I laughed sarcastically and stated, "Well, your second option is I call the cops if you do not accept my first offer." She gave me the death stare of disbelief, and analyzed my stern look to determine if I was being serious. She was at a loss for words. I continued, "Bongs, opiates, and thousands of Xanax bars." She started to threaten how bad her boyfriend would hurt me, which backfired when I stated that a threat on my life could make that an extended sentence. She quickly realized there was nothing she could do or say. She felt the energy of how serious I was, or at least how serious I looked.

She apologized and insisted I was just overreacting. She begged for a second chance, but my mind was bombarded with selfish thoughts and I felt no sympathy for her. It was not just my flawed mindset; she was also a terrible person I absolutely could not stand. After that night of my birthday I hated her. Within days, I knew why her roommate had fled, and I was ready to follow in his footsteps. With that said, I let her know my lack of sympathy for people like her. I was a drug addict, but I was still a decent human being living with a demonic psycho. I obviously was not too bothered by her drug usage, but I needed something to get out of living with such a miserable person – this was it. I decide I was going to utilize this opportunity. After I told her to make up her mind she rhetorically asked what I thought. I wrapped the confrontation up with a simple, "Okay, nice knowing you."

The room went silent for several minutes. She looked at me, grabbed her bookbag with tears rolling down her face, and tried pleading one last time for me to stop being irrational. She begged for me to accept her apology and just relax while she was walking out the door. I laughed in her face one last time and told her to have a great life. She walked out of the door unsure if this was a bluff or not. As soon as the door shut, Colton walked out of my room and screamed, "That was awesome." He continued by insisting that we grab his car to grab everything at once to be completely out before Tammy even returned back to the residence. We stuffed Colton's Civic with the few items I had. We then placed the mattress and dresser on top of his vehicle. Within twenty-five minutes, we had everything from the residence, and I was moved into the living room of The Village apartments…where my addiction would spiral out of control more than anyone thought possible.

"THE FATAL MOVE"

THIS CHAPTER'S PRIMARY PURPOSE IS to reiterate the step in addiction that loved ones would call "out of control." I prefer the term "carelessness." When I moved into this apartment, I lost all care, all morals and all sense of reality. I lost all of my natural coping abilities, as most addicts do. My natural empathic mind was eliminated, and instead I continued with my terrible egotistical mindset that had everyone on the edge of their seat. I used substances when I was stressed, sad, angry, partying, bored, and even happy. I was under the influence of substances all day, every day. Whether I was in class, a social gathering, a study group, or playing football on campus, I was always under the substance of something, or a mixture of several things.

Before I knew it I was a functioning, but nonetheless, full-blown drug addict...a complete junky. You could assume I was under the influence of something by 3:00 p.m. everyday. As soon as I got out of class I drank, did homework, drank more, and waited for Rachel to bring us the poisons for the nightly fun. This was routinized and became my daily regimen. This chapter is a summary of the last couple months leading up to my tragedy. We started my journey by going in depth with my loss of innocence, my dangerous tool of comparing and justification, and now this is the continued journey that consists of narcissism, chaos, and complete carelessness. This is the last step on the long road of my addiction, the buildup to an inevitable catastrophe. That step that will result in three places – incarceration, a hospital, or a grave. I lost all grip on reality and became careless. Careless regarding my ability to empathize with people, my future, and my existence as a whole...a completely apathetic personality.

The first week I moved into the apartment, I continued to deepen my addiction at the fastest rate I ever had. My addiction in Los Angeles was one of a saint compared to the addiction I was developing. All attributes of addiction were becoming more severe. I was drinking more heavily, smoking more often, and doing narcotics every chance I had without any sense of responsibility. The first week I moved into the apartment I consumed a mass amount of shrooms, alcohol, MDMA, cannabis, and an array of new substances, including synthetic and "testing" drugs.

This increase in consumption was no exception to the rest of this book in regards to the fact that I was walking the gloomy trail of death with my best friend, Jayden. Jayden was unofficially the new roommate at The Village apartments. He started staying at my newly claimed apartment the very first night I resided there. He rarely went back to his dorm on campus, which was roughly a mile away from the apartment. This was not necessarily a direct choice, but was a continual occurrence simply because his mind was too altered, making it physically impossible to return safely to his dorm. We would drink a twenty-four-pack each, smoked grams of marijuana in one sitting, and more than likely were under the influence of some upper. We would start our juvenile adventures directly after class, typically starting with beer and marijuana. We would eventually get to the harder substances in the evening, and would continue to participate in our devilish act until the early a.m. the next day.

My poison of choice was still LSD, but it was so hard to find near the university. I would look for it on a regular basis, but it could not be obtained by anyone. I eventually got discouraged and decided I would just adapt my drug preferences. This all goes back to the first chapter, how localities play a part in what drugs are being abused. For example, in LA I used cocaine as the primary drug of choice, which is commonly bought in bigger cities such as Los Angeles. Cocaine was not nearly as popular as MDMA was in the little college town of Radford. With that said, MDMA was the big drug that was widely accepted at the university. Even though I enjoyed the MDMA I needed to find a true hallucinogen to satisfy my need for abstract thinking and the illusions I craved so badly.

As a substitute for LSD, I decided to utilize Colton's connection in order to consume shrooms whenever I craved the hallucinogenic feeling. Colton gave me a "best friend discount" no addict could refuse. Shrooms were thirty dollars per eighth of an ounce. An eighth is the recommended dosage to successfully "trip." I paid him twenty dollars and could take from his stash as much as I wanted. This was usually four or five grams. I paid Colton forty dollars and tripped hard three days in a row the first few days I resided in the apartment. Despite that amazing deal, shrooms were not the only new substance I was abusing in the apartment. Colton also introduced me to a test drug. 2CI is a synthetic and extremely dangerous drug. It amplified all effects of an upper and mild hallucinogen to the point where it was so powerful it couldn't even be compared to the drugs it was supposed to replicate.

The first thing we did once we had all of my belongings moved into the apartment was experiment with 2CI. On the package in all caps stated: "NOT FOR HUMAN CONSUMPTION." A drug addict ignores this fact and concludes they have to put that on the label on the grounds of legalities. Colton, Jayden, and I made a gravity bong out of a plastic pitcher and a vodka bottle to experiment with the synthetic drug.

A gravity bong is home-made paraphernalia that uses the gravity and water to inhale toxins. You fill the pitcher with water and place a smaller container that has holes for the water to flow in an out of (e.g. a two-liter bottle) into the bigger container (the pitcher). You then place a metal socket or something similar to pack the drug into, and seal it to the cap of the smaller container. Once the socket is sealed to the bottle cap, you light the substance as you simultaneously slowly lift the smaller container (e.g. the two-liter bottle). When you do that smoke will rise into the smaller bottle, essentially using the laws of gravity to pull the smoke into the container. Once the gravity bong was made we were ready to try this 2CI, and what we did next truly demonstrates the common sense an addict has, or lack thereof.

Colton packed the metal socket to inhale the first rip. He inhaled the thick smoke and instantly reclined in his chair. He took a deep breath, his eyes rolled back, and he looked absolutely petrified. Jayden and I cracked up and asked him if he was okay. He replied with silence. He didn't even acknowledge the question; he just sat there and stared at his ceiling with a terrified expression. Jayden laughed as he got up to pack his rip.

He looked over at me and said, "Well, here goes nothing." He lit the concoction of the unknown synthetic chemicals. He consumed the hit with a vicious inhale. Instantly he had the same exact reaction, which didn't shock me at all. Jayden and Colton were sitting across from one another, looking at the ceiling. They both looked petrified, like they were being tormented by their own thoughts. They didn't communicate or even look at one another. Jayden and Colton had the same look, the same stiff body with one hand feeling their heart and the other in a stiff position. My addicted mind thought it looked awesome. I sprung off Colton's bed ready to proceed as the third stooge. Just as I anticipated, I went through the same process. I packed it, smoked it, and became absolutely oblivious to my surroundings and reality as an entirety.

I took my rip and immediately fell back onto Colton's bed. Within seconds I shoved my head into a pillow, and it felt as if the pillow was engulfing my face, the blanket on the bed was engulfing my body, and the drug itself was engulfing my brain. We all sat in the room terrified for our lives for nearly thirty minutes. After a couple minutes (which felt like hours) one thing made me feel better: my animated figure had shown itself once again.

The figure seemed to be the only thing I was familiar with at Radford. I was broadening my partying horizons everywhere I went. New friends, new school, new programs, new narcotics, new residence, new experiences, and a new life altogether with more substances.

One new aspect of this array of differences was the extensive party scene. The party opportunities and environments were completely foreign to me, because I was someone that was accustomed to the big-city nightlife. Radford is a college town. It is a party school that has limited bars and clubs. With that said, it has the entire social environment under the umbrella of Greek life. This is extremely common for universities that are in the middle of nowhere. We did not have fraternities at Pierce College, but Greek life surrounded Radford's campus. Our benefit was the fact that Rachel knew a brother affiliated with almost every single fraternity. She introduced us to several fraternities, and they all loved the charisma and party-animal personas Jayden and I had. Several nights a week we would drink for hours at my apartment as a pre-game to the pre-game. The legitimate pre-game was the consumption of our nightly dosage roughly forty-five minutes before going to the parties.

We had the timing to a tee. We did the drugs, specifically shrooms and MDMA, so often that we knew precisely when the effects would kick in, how long they would last, and when they would die off. Not only did we know the timing and effects of certain drug waves, but we also knew how certain substances mixed. On any given night, we would typically do MDMA and a hallucinogen that was available, which was usually shrooms. MDMA (Methylenedioxymethamphetamine) is widely known to be pure ecstasy. Essentially, it is not cut with anything. This enhances the effects significantly.

MDMA is described by the National Narcotic Division Security as –

Like other amphetamines, MDMA is a central nervous system stimulant and also hallucinogenic. On MDMA users may have a feeling of boundless energy...

Shrooms are described by the National Narcotic Division Security as –

Also known as psychedelic mushrooms, they are mushrooms that contain the psychedelic drugs psilocybin and psilocin. Effects can vary, but typically include hallucinating.

These definitions are absolutely accurate. We would utilize the mixture of these two chemicals to ensure a euphoric trip that gave us the mass amount of energy while we-party hopped the array of fraternities. This is why fraternities loved us.

Fraternities are not all bad like the media claims they are. In reality, 85% of the executives of Fortune 500 companies were Greeks. All but two of our presidents since 1825 have been Greek, and the overall Greek GPA is higher than the overall collegiate GPA. Statistically, 20% more Greeks graduate from college than do non-Greek students, and as undergraduates alone, Greeks raise over seven million dollars per year for charity. That is all I will say about that for the time being, but it is important to me that you know I am not degrading fraternities. I would never blame any entity, especially a healthy Greek life organization, for a tragedy such as addiction. In fact, Pi Lambda Phi (a social fraternity) assisted me in my recovery, but I will save that for the recovery chapter.

In conclusion, fraternities typically participate in partying, as most collegiate citizens do. These organizations didn't see two-out-of control addicts. All they saw were two extroverted individuals who were the life of the party. They never saw us sober to know the difference. Every fraternity let us into their parties knowing that we would amplify the vibes, the college environment, and of course the dancing. We rarely told the brothers what we were on, or how much we consumed, since we knew that it would probably sketch them out.

We only brought the personas that all the fraternities loved, even though they were ignorant to the fact it was merely chemical alterations that caused these personalities. We had met nearly all of the fraternities on campus. They all swarmed us with rushing and treated us exceptionally well. Jayden and I knew that we had interest in rushing a fraternity; we just didn't know which one, or if we were ready to give up the drug usage for community service and academic study hours. When they informed us of those fraternal obligations we could not help but to think "drugs>Greek life." Long story short, rush week was coming up in a few days and we both agreed we would stay unaffiliated for the time being. Days after rush week was over we did not feel the same welcoming environment we had before. Many fraternities felt we just reaped the benefits, but refused to join. They were correct. This directly resulted in broadening our horizons even more. We decided to look elsewhere for our nightly festivities.

There was a new fraternity on campus that was not very publicized yet. I still had no intentions of rushing, but I figured I might as well grow my social network. I thought that no rushing conversations would occur due to the fact rush week was over, but sure enough the topic was brought up. We were enlightened on something call a "snap bid." Before the conversation got too in depth we respectfully declined their offer of a "snap bid," which they said was an invitation to membership that is given to an individual after the traditional rush week is over. Despite the fact that it sparked our interest, we kindly refused their offer. To our surprise, the fraternity was still extremely respectful to Jayden and me.

This fact was an eye-opener about their personalities, intentions, values, and morals. This resulted with the two of us wanting to go nowhere else but Pi Lambda Phi. One night after our daily dose of substances, we found ourselves at the prospering fraternity's house once again. We could easily assume that they were not nearly as wild or popular as the rest of them, but they were the most respectable group of men we had ever met. We discussed how they seemed to have no hidden motives like the rest of the fraternities. Whether we pledged the fraternity or not, they enjoyed us being at their parties. In fact, they were so welcoming that I drunkenly told them that I had consumed nearly an 8-ball of cocaine with Jayden the night I was at their party. They gave me advice that would be a huge reality slap to most people, but to an addict it was a "low blow." They told me that they knew I was having substance-abuse issues, and that they knew that was stopping me from pledging. I glared at the brothers with an offended expression. One brother, Wilson, even stated that if I ever wanted a bid I would have to stop the drug abuse. He continued by stating it was not something the fraternity approved of, and it could personally get me in a lot of trouble. He was very respectful and subtle, but regardless of his politeness I was offended. I slammed my cup and stormed out of the fraternity's house.

When I woke up, despite the uncalled outburst, a brother of Pi Lambda Phi's organization called me at 7:00 a.m. with horrific news. "Jayden's been arrested," the brother said. I woke up with drool rolling down my face and moaned back into the phone. The brother repeated himself a bit louder and reality hit me harder than the hangover. I sprang off of the couch that I'd drunkenly fallen asleep on. It wasn't strange that I was on the couch, because I lived in the living room. What caught me by surprise was the fact that I was not alone. I looked in the mirror feeling disgusted; I had woken up lying with Rachel. I hung up the phone with the brother and had no idea where to start...

I raced to the bathroom and vomited. It must have been the disgust from the mixture of the alcohol and the fact I woke up next to a girl who wasn't Stephanie. I knew I had to deal with Rachel as she was in a dead sleep on my couch, but before I dealt with that issue I had to make sure Jayden was not in the New River Valley Jail. I went to see if he was sleeping anywhere in the apartment. I thought maybe the police had dropped him off, but he was nowhere in the apartment or the dorm. I frantically made calls to a plethora of peers that we were with the night before. Jayden's dormmates hadn't heard from him, Rachel hadn't spoken to him, or anyone else for that matter. I could not find anyone from the party but the brother who'd called me claiming they had seen him.

I finally called one of our buddies named Justin. Justin was the only one who was there until the party ended, and he told me that he'd witnessed Jayden being arrested right outside of the fraternity house. I called the inmate lookup service and they confirmed that Jayden was in custody. His charges were underage possession of alcohol and being drunk in public. Thank the Lord the fifteen-year-sentence's worth of drugs were at the apartment. I called Jake, Tammy's friend, to give me a ride to the jail to bail him out before he was forced to call his parents. Jake was still up from the night before and agreed to give me a ride to the jail without hesitation. He jokingly stated, "Hell yeah, bro. It happens to the best of us."

I called the correctional institution, telling them to notify Jayden I was on my way before he could regrettably notify his parents. While Jake was getting ready to come grab me to go to the jail, I decided it was time to confront the other issue, Rachel. I gave Rachel a subtle shake to wake her up. She opened her eyes and gave me a sweet good morning. Ignoring the sweet talk, I frantically asked her what had happened, what did we do, and furthermore did we do anything sexual. She informed me in a seductive voice that I was having no part in sex because of my "b**** a** girlfriend," but that she sure attempted. I laughed and took a deep breath of relief. She gave me a death-stare and slowly sat up.

She asked who I was on the phone with. I informed her of where Jayden was, how he got there, and the situation we found ourselves in the night prior... I blamed myself for causing the scene and leaving in the first place. I continued by telling her that Jake was on his way to take me to the jail in order to bail him out. She rolled her eyes, laughed, and laid her head down and was back unconscious within minutes.

Jake pulled up to the apartment parking lot, I hopped into his eighties Buick, and we drove down Interstate 81 to go retrieve Jayden from the New River Valley Jail. Once we got there, it took hours for them to process the paperwork and release our friend. The correctional officers were rude, almost if they knew I should be in their custody. After dealing with the magistrate, correctional officers, and other officials with enormous egos I finally got to see my best friend. He looked absolutely terrible when he walked out of the secured doors separating us from the inmates. I felt so bad for my best friend words could not describe it. If anyone belonged in a jail cell it was me, and I knew that. I felt completely responsible for the situation, because we'd developed an implied buddy system.

This buddy system was never officially stated, but as many youngsters do, we both assumed we would always leave parties together to ensure events like this wouldn't happen. With that said, I felt like I'd failed him as a best friend. The first time I broke this "bro-code" Jayden got arrested, and for that, I felt like a miserable person. Due to my anger issues I'd stormed out of the fraternity's house, resulting in Jayden walking back to the apartment alone. After I gave Jayden my sincere apologizes, I let him know that Rachel was cooking us food so he could have a nutritional meal when we arrived back at the apartment. He sarcastically laughed and asked, "What about alcohol?"

You are probably thinking to yourself that most individuals would not drink after this for an undetermined but considerable amount of time. In fact, some would debate ever drinking again after getting arrested. Obviously, someone with their head on straight would quit after being incarcerated, realizing that drinking hindered their well-being. An addict, on the other hand, will try to justify what happened so they do not have to blame their metaphorical abuser. I knew Jayden was not going to give up drinking, which is exactly why my answer to his question was, "Hell yes, man. I have a bottle of vodka with your name on it at the house."

After Jayden got arrested, we decided to make some changes so we would never have to deal with the authorities again. We figured we could simply turn the apartment into a party house itself. We jokingly agreed that we had more alcohol, fun, and girls than the fraternities combined anyway. We figured this would kick all of our problems to the curb. Our minds were corrupted by addiction, and we figured if we didn't leave the apartment we couldn't do anything wrong…or at least be caught doing anything wrong. All of our friends, including Colton, Alex, and our buddy Justin, were all for the change of pace. We all were content with the apartment being the new 24/7 substance house.

Another benefit of doing that was the fact that Justin was loaded and could afford to satisfy just about all of our addictions by buying the supply from Rachel and me. Not just was Justin loaded, but he was also extremely generous with his money and the drugs he always purchased. He was also in the military, which spawned the same constraints on partying that Alex had. With that said, just like Alex, smoking marijuana was not an option for him due to the fact that it can appear on a drug test even after a month of prior usage. The military has random screening for the reserves every time they meet for drill, therefore a month to "get clean" is difficult. The difference between Justin and Alex was the fact that alcohol was not enough to satisfy Justin's desire to have an altered mindset. This caused Justin's addicted mind to be sent on a journey to find another substance that could satisfy his desires, but also have a chemical compound that could be flushed out quickly.

Fortunately for him this journey was not a difficult one. Most addicts are aware that an array of drugs, including MDMA, can be flushed out of your system within a day. It only takes as little as twenty-four hours for many substances to be considered untraceable. Justin fell in love with that fact, and furthermore fell in love with MDMA. To accompany that burning love of MDMA, he wanted his friends to feel that same admiration for the drug. He wanted it to be socially and mutually loved. In other words, to make it socially acceptable. With that said, he would buy everyone MDMA in the apartment, meaning Rachel and I could buy it in bulk. Several nights of the week he would spend hundreds of dollars for him and everyone else in the apartment to do mass amounts of MDMA.

Rachel, on the other hand, hated the change in our nightlife, although she enjoyed the loads of free MDMA. She was a big partier. She enjoyed being the center of attention at fraternities. She would still go out and was sure to invite me out with her every night, but I would kindly decline in favor of hanging out at the apartment. It turned into a daily routine of her accessing the drugs, bringing them to the apartment, snorting them with us, and then begging me to go out with her. It was a very rare occurrence that I would actually go with her, but that did not stop her from trying every chance she had.

After a few weeks it finally became apparent to her that I was content with staying at the apartment from the night's beginning to end. All I wanted was to be under the influence, and if I was I would be satisfied with just staying at the apartment. It drove her insane that I was playing this "hard to get game" with her. For the most part, it was because I truly wanted to be at the apartment, but there was a side of the situation that you could consider a game of "hard to get." Better yet, because of Stephanie, it was a game of impossible to get.

This is exactly what drove Rachel's extreme interest in me. I was the only guy that was in her network of people that she wanted but could not have. The more I ignored her interest in me, the more she was desperate for my attention. Most individuals are fascinated with what they cannot obtain. With that said, her interest in me and my lack of attention toward her correlated perfectly. When Jayden and I first made our "responsible" decision to become homebound she would still go out for hours, trying her hardest to not adapt to our change in plans. She acted as if she wanted no part of it, but I knew deep down it was bothering her that she couldn't manipulate the two of us. Manipulation is a huge attribute of addicts, but it was difficult for her to manipulate my addicted mind. It is hard to manipulate a manipulator.

She figured that we would eventually come out of our shell and return to the wild parties. She assumed that after a few short nights of missing out on the fun we would return to our old habits. She eventually came to the realization that she couldn't be more wrong. After a couple weeks went by, she came to the conclusion that we were not budging. The new daily routine started with her bringing the drugs to the apartment, leaving the residence, and then being back within the same hour. She was desperate for my attention, but I was still loyal to Stephanie. She would try to manipulate me by expressing what parties she was missing out on because she wanted to spend the night with me, but I refused to give in. I was still living the values and morals that were instilled in me since early childhood. I was not a cheater! For the time being, my last grasp on reality was still there, and I knew Rachel was no good for my well-being.

The fact that I would not break up with, or cheat on, Stephanie drove her crazy. To try to gradually capture my attention, her "nights on the town" were declining while her feelings for me became blatant. Her "hard to get" game was diminished, and she would consistently tell everyone how bad she wanted my attention. This resulted in her adapting to our homebody plans, and the rare times that she would go out resulted in her return within thirty minutes. She eventually knew all she wanted to do with her time every night of the week was spend it with us two buffoons.

My attention, or lack thereof, was not the only thing driving Rachel up the wall. She was also driven to insanity by her attraction to our wildness. My rebellion, deviance, and wild-boy attitude was a huge turn on for her. This being the base of a relationship was not good, and I comprehended that. This ultimately was the reason I knew she was no good for me, even though the temptation of such a wild relationship was definitely there. Alex, Jayden, and Justin were following me in my crazy night festivities. When we stopped the typical college party life we entered a whole new level of deviance and chaos. Every night was a new wild story similar to the high school nights I spent with Jayden.

Stealing, fighting, and even running from police was at least a weekly occurrence. For example, some nights when I was obliterated I would decide that I didn't want to spend money on beer. I was an expert at stealing single beers and Four Locos from high school, but taking twenty-four ounces of alcohol and sticking it in my pants wasn't going to get the job done anymore. My craving for intoxication and tolerance became way too strong for that. With that said, I would walk into the closest local grocery store, grab a case or two, and sprint out of the store.

Simple as that…if I was caught, I would keep sprinting. It was such a flawless operation that some nights I would come back with at least six cases after hitting two or three stores. I was known for this insane stunt that I would do at least once a week. This was an activity that I picked up in high school, and I would continue to increase the amount of alcohol as it correlated with the severity of my addiction and carelessness. This wasn't the only habit I continued from high school. We would obliterate mailboxes, signs, and other public property. We completely demolished public property just as we had in high school. This bad habit also grew out of control, just like everything else did. It only got worse, riskier, and more chaotic as our care for our well-being declined.

To put this in perspective, one night I kicked over an entire banister in front of someone's home. The ironic part of the whole adventure is that I was by myself. I had no influence, dares, or reason beside the fact I was in a rage. I was walking back from across campus where I had just bought some cocaine. It was through people outside our direct network, therefore I was the only one going. I left the house that I was at around 5:00 p.m. As I was walking back, I saw a front-porch banister belonging to someone who'd skimped us on some MDMA. It looked as if it had suffered from wood rot for years. I walked up to the residence, to the banister, and brutally kicked it three or four times until I had the fifty-pound banister completely detached from the porch. I grabbed the banister in broad daylight and walked it back to my apartment that was a block away. I stumbled up the steps to the apartment and swung the door open. Everyone stared at me in disbelief as I screamed, "We won that war, and here is our trophy."

We used that banister to document the wild stories, quotes, and theories we had while we were under the influence. We wrote our "brain cells" theory I described previously on the banister. Jayden followed that thought by writing a theory on planets. He went into detail about what planets had which personalities. These were the first two items written on the banister. Following those wild theories people signed the banister, wrote funny quotes people said under the influence, wrote chaotic experiences in the apartment, and described in writing the other hilarious occurrences while we were under the influence. When something remarkably hysterical happened, it would be sure to make it "on the banister."

Some of those stories included the morning we woke up to human feces in our washer, Alex's logic on the biology of broccoli, and our famous saying we would always scream while under the influence, "Too much serotonin in my brain." Another section consisted of a tally of the times when Alex and I would kick everyone out the apartment to fist-fight one another about things as stupid as video games, or how many hours the flight took from Virginia to China.

One of the most out-of-control stories written on the banister explained the night Alex and I drove a CAT tractor. We were operating the tractor until campus security spotted us. The officer knocked on the driver-side door, where Alex was operating the tractor. Alex turned the machinery off, looked at me, and told me to open my side of the tractor. My glare back implied I knew he was planning on booking it. I replied with the words, "YOU ARE NUTS!!" As the campus security guy continued yelling from outside the tractor, he asked me if going to jail was in my plans for the night. I immediately swung the door open, jumped to the ground running, and sprinted all the way back to our apartment laughing hysterically.

My reason for giving you this insight is not to brag. If I wanted to brag, I would need to write a book of stories the size of *Moby-Dick*. This is only a fraction of my experiences that I am willing to share. To be honest, to this day, I am ashamed that I was so out of control. The reason for briefly going over these chaotic experiences is that it is necessary to understand what true carelessness is before I continue giving the rest of my journey of addiction.

People can get arrested for a variety of things that could be worth the small risk of being caught. Obviously, smoking marijuana in your bedroom before bed probably will not result in a legal battle. Having sex in a position that is not missionary is a common crime as well in certain states, but the risk and severity is so low most people are not worried about it. Individuals who do such miniscule crimes typically CARE about their life. Even if an individual were to commit an illegal act, such as speeding, they evaluate the risks and severity of what act they are committing. If you have a sexual encounter that is not missionary position, you realize and evaluate that the risk is almost nonexistent and it is not hurting anyone. My point is most individuals analyze the risk, severity of deviance, and punishment before they act. Simply put, they CARE about their personal longevity and happiness. On the other hand, an individual who does cocaine in a public institution is probably an addict, and furthermore is CARELESS about the bigger picture. The risk is so great, the reward is so miniscule, but an addict does not care. They are not able to see the bigger picture, because the drug has their mind restrained.

The second point I want to reiterate is how much Rachel fell in love with my wild side. She loved this persona, but this persona was not actually me. This persona became more prevalent in day-to-day interactions as my drug consumption increased. She desperately tried to be with me, and as I was losing my grasp on reality I wanted to be with her as well.

One night, my morals and sobriety standards dropped below my level of intoxication and temptation. We were under the influence of a lot of alcohol accompanied by a large dosage of MDMA, and at nineteen years old I cheated for the first time. The buildup of temptation viciously released itself all at once on Rachel's lips. We ripped one another's clothes off as if they were on fire. I threw her on the couch, in a sexual way of course, and lay on top of her. She looked at me with a look of accomplishment. Emotions were through the roof. As we finally gave in to the temptation of our first sexual encounter, I looked at the ceiling and lifted myself off the couch. I started into Rachel's eyes and knew I was about to do something absolutely terrible. I got up and took a deep breath with my hands placed above my head. I was distraught and silent.

After a few moments, she abruptly broke the silence by frantically interrogating me about what I was doing. My conscience kicked in at the very last minute. It was able to stop me, and I apologized, stating that I couldn't do it. She was angry, but continued to lie on the couch with the vibe that she was not going to take no for an answer. She continued by stating that I could at least cuddle with her for screwing with her head so much. I agreed to her request after a minute of contemplation. I still felt terrible, but I felt I hadn't necessarily cheated. The addict in me justified my actions by telling myself I could easily have had sex, but I was able to resist the burning desire…and trust me, the desire was burning. I compared myself, as addicts do, to most college guys that I knew who would have given in a long time ago. In conclusion, I overcame the temptation. I was proud of myself for that, but the temptation grew to an entire new level after I tasted a dose of Rachel's toxic love.

It took no time at all to be defeated by the deadly temptation. With that said, I tried to do the right thing by attempting to end my current relationship with Stephanie. I wanted to clear my conscience of cheating by doing this, but Stephanie used guilt and threats, which prevented me from making the right decision of ending our intimate relationship. She had the accurate gut feeling that my reason was another girl, but I denied it by claiming I simply needed a break due to the stress of distance. I felt bad for lying, but not nearly as bad as I felt for cheating. She interrogated the hell out of me about my reasoning until I backed out of my intention of breaking up with her. She continued by threatening that she would never speak to me again if I were to follow through with the breakup, knowing it was for another girl, although I would not confirm that.

After those conversations, a gram of MDMA, and forty-eight hours later, I decided I could not lose Stephanie from my life. Ultimately, this resulted in me participating in the devilish game of cheating. Rachel and I took care of the unfinished business shortly after my phone call with Stephanie. I felt terrible, but the sexual encounters that Rachel and I engaged in were the best ones I ever had. Rachel was extremely wild in and out of bed, and I loved it. We engaged in all sorts of exotic positions, adventurous places, and various angles. There is no need to go too in depth, but the bottom line is something terrible happened. I got addicted to Rachel. My devilish, addictive personality applied to Rachel just as it did to drugs, but my addiction to her happened instantly. Starting from our first intimate engagement, we were both hooked...

The sex was so wild and loud that it woke Jayden up in the other room. Jayden did not confront us the night it happened for obvious reasons, but he confronted me the next morning. The look he gave me on my birthday as he noticed me gazing at Rachel was explained the morning following the sexual encounter. He told me Rachel's current standing in her health, personality, and legal troubles. He started by telling me that Rachel had a very rational fear of having hepatitis C. In fact, she was almost positive she had it. She was afraid to get tested, but probability stated the disease was spreading through her veins. I did some online research and came to the conclusion that this disease is rarely transmitted through sex, but spreads through the share of needles...I was confused.

He continued telling me that Rachel was in the process of trying to kick heroin, but I knew that. She'd been addicted to her love of heroin for nearly three years. She knew I couldn't inject myself with a needle, but I had no issue with the drug itself. Secondly, she would never put me in danger by sharing her equipment, ultimately exposing me to the hepatitis C if she had it. I didn't judge her for it, and even found it somewhat attractive that she was as crazy as I.

Jayden told me about her plans to attend a rehabilitation center in New Jersey. This was something that I was also aware of, and something I was proud of her for. Everyone in America loves a come-up story. My addicted mindset did not find the obvious contradiction in doing drugs with someone who planned to go to rehab, but that is another example of the blindfold your "abuser" has wrapped around your head. "I don't do heroin. I am not contributing to her issues." Although I knew about her intention of going to rehab, I was not aware of her reasoning. I figured that she was doing it for herself, her longevity, and to finally kick heroin. I could not be more wrong.

Her primary reason was not for sobriety, but purely to avoid prison time. She was facing up to four years for possession of narcotics with the intent to distribute. This absolutely terrified her. She never told me this, because she felt I would discontinue our relationship if I knew that she was involved with the police, as I had with other friends and acquaintances. Her lawyer told her it was a necessity to attend a rehabilitation center to prevent a Virginia judge from "throwing the book" at her.

She utilized her professional, and extremely expensive, legal advice. Her father was paying for it and wanted her to go immediately, but she somehow delayed the rehabilitation process with her father's approval. Jayden explained to me that she was waiting until the summer, and that was something else I did not have answers for. I did not comprehend why she was delaying the process, because she was not in school and had a job at a local restaurant. Jayden finally concluded by saying, "I don't know much more than that. She didn't want me telling you this, but you are my best friend." He concluded, "She is no good for you, man, just keep your relationship in the friend zone. The least you can do for yourself is confront her on these things so she can tell you for herself, and you can make your decision from there."

That is exactly what I did. She was honest, too honest for my comfort. We were under the influence of MDMA mixed with a tad bit of cocaine, but this was not a euphoric high. We were extremely high, because we attempted to ease the pain of the conversation we knew was getting ready to take place. She was comfortable with being so brutally honest, because, like most addicts, she used the dangerous tool of justification and the drug itself to ease the anxiety. We sat outside of the apartment building and discussed her life until the sun came up.

She told me she was pretty sure she had hepatitis C, but justified it with the fact that it was curable and was not sexually transmitted. She came clean about the sentence as well, but also used excuses and justification to make it seem like no big deal. She claimed it was a big misunderstanding. She said she was caught with two pills over the summer before school. I asked where the intention to distribute came into play with such a miniscule amount. She informed me that they were bagged in separate baggies, and I could not comprehend how she got in the middle of this "misunderstanding." She claimed that this was the reason she was charged with intent to distribute, and although I found this hard to believe I gave her the benefit of the doubt.

We moved onto the next hardship that was a result of her addicted self-destruction. She attempted to lay her reason for delaying rehab on me. She told me she was not ready to leave me and she was falling in love. I had to object to her reasoning, and demanded that she stop stringing me along. She then came clean and stated that she could not go to rehab at the moment, because her father believed that she was still attending school. That begged further questions. It left me with many assumptions that could only be confirmed by her.

Even though the assumptions were not confirmed, I wanted it to stay that way. I had put two and two together and was ashamed I was falling for such a person. It all made sense how she was affording to buy copious amounts of drugs, pay her bills, and have the money to go on shopping sprees for the both of us whenever she wanted. She claimed she was making great tips at work, but the restaurant was far from upper class. The fact of the matter was that she was using "tuition" money from her father on all of those unnecessary things. A typical person would realize this was a self-destructive girl who was running into issues everywhere. They would come to the conclusion that this person should not be associated with, let alone a girlfriend.

I thought of myself as a young man with a promising future, but that was my "abuser" justifying the fact that I was just as bad. The depressing truth was I became that same self-destructive individual that she was. You are the average of the five people you hang out with the most. Her self-inflicted misery was bringing hardship in regards to health, education, and the law, and it was reflecting onto me, subconsciously deepening my self-destructive tendencies. As an addict myself, I didn't have the perspective that I should have on the situation. Just as I did with my metaphorical "abuser," I justified my new addiction, Rachel. I knew she was hindering my life, putting me at high risk, and just like with a drug, I could not stop even on those sufficient grounds.

The cheating, lying, and deception continued. I was spiraling into something I never thought I would be. I was a junky by the start of the second month I was attending Radford. I was a cheater, skipping class, being violent, and neglected my girlfriend Stephanie. I was tempting her to break up with me by blatantly ignoring her for days at a time. I figure I would cheat, ignore her until she broke up with me, and then do enough substances that I didn't even feel bad for it.

With that said, I cheated, and I cheated a lot. The heart grief became so bad that I would completely neglect Stephanie so I did not have to face the man in the mirror every time I heard her voice. During the week I may have called her once or twice. She would call Jayden, but as any good friend would, he covered for me. He is in class, he is playing lacrosse, and he lost his phone were the three big excuses to minimize the suspicion. This is ironic because I rarely went to class, rarely went outside, and always was on the phone with drug dealers.

Stephanie was fed up with how "busy" my life was and demanded that I make a trip to Kingsdale. I agreed, thinking that was what I needed to rekindle my morals, values, relationships, and ultimately get back on track. With that said, Jayden and I drove to Kingsdale to go visit Stephanie and Katlyn. Stephanie wanted me to come up that weekend specifically because of a celebration she wanted me to be a part of. Stephanie had pledged a sorority and her initiation party was taking place the same night we got in. Stephanie asked her sisterhood if the few of us coming from out of town could attend the party. She received approval with the condition that we were aware we would be the only two guys that were not a part of the fraternity that was co-sponsoring the social gathering. With that said, the initiation party consisted of one fraternity, Stephanie's sorority, Katlyn, and the two Radford nuisances.

Over the course of the night, Stephanie noticed the negative attitude change in me. Instead of drinking like a college student, I drank like I was seeking a suicidal BAC. Instead of smoking marijuana, I insisted she find me MDMA or cocaine as Rachel did. She was confused about why I was acting the way I was, but she just brushed these personality differences off. We did not find any drugs, but Jayden and I did successfully down a bottle of Jose each before we went out. We got to the fraternity party and felt uncomfortable being the only two non-affiliates in the fraternity's house. We decided to take a trip to the convenience store a couple blocks from the house to go steal some beer.

We walked down to the store talking about how dumb the party was, and how we both badly wished we'd stayed in Radford. All I could think about was how bad I wanted to be back at our apartment

– furthermore, how bad I wanted to be back with Rachel. I was at the point where I could not stand being with Stephanie. In fact, when we tried to sleep together it was impossible for me to do so. I ultimately was at the point where I needed to end the relationship, but every time I tried I couldn't. She had been my best friend my whole later years of childhood. I didn't know what to do. It was love vs. lust, right vs. wrong, and with the corrosive substances I couldn't see the blatant answer I was looking for. Part of me may have been holding back due to the fact that deep down I knew Stephanie would truly be the healthier and more beneficial person to be in a relationship with. I used the walk to the convenience store to dump those feelings on Jayden.

He was speechless, and his mind was just as corroded from drugs as mine. He gave generic best-friend advice. Something along of the lines of "follow your heart" or "do what makes you happy." The answer to both of those questions, at that moment, were drugs and Rachel. I finished the emotional rant by asking if we could leave tomorrow instead of Sunday evening. Jayden decided that it was completely okay, because of how incredibly boring we found Kingsdale.

We wrapped up our conversation, stole our beers, and went back to the fraternity house. We stood in the corner awkwardly as we had before we left to go to the convenience store. Jayden and I were in the same uncomfortable position we were in before, but we figured at least we did not have to wait for beer anymore. We hung out and minded our own business until one of the fraternity brothers came and took Jayden's beer from his hand and threw it away. Jayden instantly pushed him against the wall, slapped the red Solo cup out of his hand, and demanded another beer. In shock from Jayden's drunken outburst, the fraternity brother went to go get Jayden another beer. He must not have seen mine, or else had a personal vendetta against Jayden.

When he came back with a Solo cup of beer, he apologized to Jayden. As Jayden freaked out, the fraternity brother was in the middle of explaining that "outside" alcohol was prohibited. This was purely a safety precaution, but neither of us would accept that answer. Jayden viciously slapped the Solo cup out of his hand again and screamed, "I had a can of beer! Not a cup, you A-hole." The verbal argument between Jayden and the other gentleman had quickly escalated. He demanded Jayden leave, and Jayden demanded he made him. A few of the brothers caught sight of Jayden's rampage and started migrating toward us. They were multiplying. Jayden and I were back to back, anticipating one of the brothers starting a physical fight. Stephanie and Katlyn were nowhere to be found.

They must have been enjoying the party like everyone else was until Jayden and I abruptly ended the good vibes. The verbal argument inside quickly escalated into an enormous physical altercation outside. It was about thirty vs. two as we got into a shoving match with the four or five brothers that stepped to the plate first. The rest of the brothers stood behind the ones that were ready for combat, waiting for Jayden or me to strike first. Jayden and I had egos that skyrocketed so high we weren't going to back down. Jayden was pushed and told to leave before he got his "a** whooped." Jayden respond exactly how I expected he would, and socked the individual who'd slapped the beer out of his hand in the left cheek.

Brothers broke it up and gave us an ultimatum. We could either leave the premises or be jumped. The mind said flight, the alter-ego said fight, and that falsified ego won once again. As Jayden and I ran with our fists cocked back, a cop passed the fraternity's residence. He stopped and asked what was taking place. A sober fraternity brother was able to convince him we were all playing around. He explained it was an initiation celebration and the officer left without further questioning. As the police officer was leaving, only giving us a simple warning, Stephanie sprinted outside to diffuse the situation before someone was arrested or hospitalized.

We went back to her dormitory, where we started a fight of our own. I was in a drunken rage, and I claimed she cared about the fraternity more than me. In hindsight I probably was expressing the anger with myself and transferring that onto Stephanie. Stephanie was a victim of my cheating, the real reason I was so angry, but at the time I saw her as at fault for the cheating. Once again, the addict justifying themself.

I couldn't tell her I was cheating, and this was my way of expressing the anger built up from the whole situation. My tensions with Stephanie escalated and got Jayden all hyped up. Now Jayden and I both were in a drunken outrage, which resulted in a threat of leaving Kingsdale immediately. We stormed down the staircase. When we entered Jayden's vehicle it became apparent that Jayden was too intoxicated for a four-hour drive back to Radford. It took him nearly ten minutes to unlock his vehicle. With that said, we slept in Jayden's car and left early in the morning before anyone woke up to stop us. We justified leaving because of the fight, but in hindsight it was merely an excuse to spend the rest of the weekend in our own wild way, in our apartment, with our substances. All I wanted was to be on my time, with my drugs, and with my new love, Rachel.

We returned to the sanctuary that Saturday night. Before I entered the apartment building, I called Stephanie. I kept this phone call short, simple, and to the point. I told her I needed a break, and nothing she could do or say would change that. She finally accepted with no hesitation, lifting the weight of a mistress and a hellish affair off my shoulders. I was apathetic about the whole situation, and she was distraught. I wiped my hands clean, and figured "no harm, no foul." When I finished the phone call, I started walking toward my apartment to tell Jayden I had finally "taken care of it." When I walked into the apartment, I noticed that Alex was extremely intoxicated. It was not like a normal "Alex drunk." Alex was absurd, obnoxious, and out of control.

Even I could attest to the fact that he was too intoxicated, which should put it in perspective. When Alex would depart for drill he would typically return with moonshine. On the nights when he would grab a couple of moonshine jars to consume he would reach a new level of intoxication that everyone hated. The nights we would binge drink moonshine were almost always the nights that Alex and I would be involved in physical altercations. Anyway, the night that we got back to Radford he had downed an entire mason jar of toxic moonshine. Rachel met us at the apartment, and when she arrived, Alex had no idea who she was.

We had moved the party out in front of the apartment when Alex kindly asked Rachel her name. Keep in mind that Rachel was at our apartment every day, meaning that Alex saw her several times a day. We laughed at Alex, thinking he was just drunkenly attempting to be comical. He asked again with a tone of confusion and frustration, as if he could not comprehend why we were all ignoring the question. We all stared at him in disbelief when he screamed, "I am just going to call you Jamaica until you tell me your real name." She was wearing a Rastafarian drug rug, which was his reasoning behind the statement he thought was comical. We could not believe he was serious. Jayden eventually got just as intoxicated as Alex. He was trying to climb the balconies of the apartment building. The bottom line was, the apartment crew was in an oblivious state of intoxication. Rachel and I were not sober by any means, but we did have a different altered mind state than the rest of our buddies. Rachel and I were under the influence of downers with a bit of MDMA in the mix so we didn't have the same ridiculous, obnoxious, and insane drunk humor as everyone else. To say the least, it was annoying us to no end. I also had important news to tell her, so I figured this would be the perfect time to do so.

With that said, we decided to flee the scene and make our own party. We decided we would go on an adventure with just the two of us. We got off the curb and started walking towards Rachel's vehicle. I had her keys in my hand as I walked toward the driver-side door. As I swung the door open, I heard Jayden sprinting behind me. He grabbed the back of my shirt and started begging us not to drive. Jayden was being a good friend and saw how dangerous it was. He interrogated us on where we had to go that was so important, how intoxicated we were, and what he could do to stop us. He was dealing with two manipulative individuals. It was not too complicated to assure Jayden that everything would be okay.

We convinced him that we were both fine and completely coherent. The amount of MDMA that I had been ingesting gave me an invincible and careless mindset that truly made me believe that I was okay to drive. After about fifteen minutes, Jayden was content with letting us leave. He hesitantly told us to have a good time whatever we were going to do. I shook Jayden's hand and jumped in Rachel's vehicle.

As we pulled out of the complex, we realized we had no destination, mission, or reason to drive. I drove toward the back roads of Radford as Rachel kicked her shoes off and put her feet out of the window. She wanted to go on a journey that had no end. She told me to drive wherever I wanted. We got on Interstate 81, and as we accelerated up the ramp I literally felt a wave of invincibility correlating with the increasing speed. I didn't realize I was doing exactly what Robert had done in L.A. I felt as if I was in a game of *GTA*, free of trouble, punishment, or consequence. It seemed it was all mere imagination. If a cop were to flash his lights, I told Rachel I was going to book it, and she was fine with it. The revving engine, blowing wind, and loud music put us in euphoria. The euphoric feeling made it impossible to think about any potential consequence.

As I increased my speed up the freeway, my adrenaline was rising at a rapid pace. My invincible mindset had never hit such a magnitude. The speedometer was rising through 40, 50, 60, 70, 80, and then started to fall to the right, reaching 90, 100, 110, 120, and eventually we reached 140 mph. I have never driven so fast at a consistent speed in my life. I loved it. We got about 40 miles away from Radford in no time... It was unbelievable. After the insane pursuit, we turned back around to head to the apartment. I was extremely fortunate that I avoided being arrested, dying, or killing someone else. The invincible mindset overpowered my common sense and logic.

This is just a summary of the months leading up to my tragedy. The next chapter is what everyone has been waiting for, the overdose that nearly cost me my life. The weekend my overdose happened was similar to the previous binges I have explained. With that said, there is no need to explain an identical weekend to the rest of them. The only differences were the magnitude of carelessness, the amount of intoxication, the fact I didn't sleep for days, and that Jayden was not there to keep me under control, which you see he did A LOT. It was a weekend that entailed me being high for days on several drugs with absolutely no sleep, and neglecting the potential deadly consequences of my decisions. Three days before I overdosed I skipped every class, I drank heavily with Justin all day (typically with Xanax to ensure we blacked out), split 8-balls of cocaine with Rachel day after day, and partied relentlessly all night long with my polysubstance abuse issues.

It started with a typical Friday night that resulted with me staying up through that Saturday morning. It was about 8:00 a.m. on Saturday when I realized I still had a criminal justice assignment I needed to do before Monday. With that said, I took 120 mg of Vyvanse in order to concentrate on the assignment. Rachel had to work until that Saturday afternoon so I figured this was when I would do my homework. I knew that my body needed sleep, but I figured that it would be a quick fix with more uppers. I had no distractions, so I figured this would be the perfect time to complete my obligations. Colton hadn't been around, Jayden had gone back home, and Alex was at drill with the National Guard. Everyone else in Radford was sleeping off their hangover. With that said, by the time I had completed my assignment I'd been up for about forty hours or so. When Rachel returned from work, I was ready to sleep. I had taken several barbiturates that Jake had sold me in order to counteract the uppers I had been taking. As I was finally falling asleep, Rachel ran through the apartment door filled with excitement.

She used the guilt of her long day at work in order to convince me into staying up with her, but I knew I needed a chemical in order to do that. With that said, I continued my two-day binge of Vyvanse, MDMA, cocaine, and Rachel's new connection to crack. This kept me wide awake through the whole weekend, counteracting the tranquil state that I was in from the drugs Jake had sold me. I was in oblivion from lack of sleep, a confused heart rate, and the most intensive drug binge of my life. We spent hundreds of dollars, our hearts and minds were weak, and we had been up over seventy-two hours on drugs. We stayed in the apartment for three days doing drugs on the binge from hell. Jayden came back to Radford that Sunday and had no idea what I had been doing, that I had now gotten into crack, how long I'd been up, or the inevitable tragic collapse he was about to witness.

"THE OVERDOSE"

BEFORE I CONTINUE TO EXPLAIN how my final drug binge ended, I want to reiterate my addiction process. Remember when I said it is necessary to understand the journey to addiction, not just the tragedy. The journey of addiction is as complex and drawn-out as the recovery process. Consequently, I have given an in-depth insight into how my addiction started. This process started with my loss of innocence, continued by explaining how my addiction arose due to what became socially acceptable, followed by how it deepened with justification and comparison, and how finally it rose to the climatic peak accompanied by carelessness.

The metaphorical "abuser" made me its mindless sheep. It would soon take everything from me. Stephanie, friends, and reality would soon just be a figment of my past life. These beneficial attributes of my life were replaced by physical altercations, an unhealthy mistress, and a new altered egotistical jerk that became the "real me" before I was able to stop it. I became an individual who always strived to live off the impulse of danger and drugs. I was in a role conflict. I knew who I was deep down, but I knew what person the drugs had brought to life even better. It's like the drugs brought to life that animation figure, me as the devil.

I now had become that animation my mind spawned during my LSD trips, and I couldn't stop it from happening. I had the addictive personality, and at this point in time I couldn't control my urge for drugs. Essentially, I was living two opposite lives. I was living the two lives of a college student vs. a druggie, a virtuous man vs. an apathetic rebel, and living in a love trio with Stephanie and Rachel. I was living a life that was a consistent battle between me and my ego.

It only took about three months in Radford to reach this peak with drugs, rebellion, and the role conflict of my ego itself. I was a prospering college student, but I was up till the wee hours under the influence of drugs nearly every night. I would sleep a maximum of three hours the nights that I would even allow my body to sleep at all. When I decided to attend class, it was only possible with the use of Cocaine, Vyvanse, or Adderall. It was at the point where I could not get out of bed unless I had at least 60 mg of Adderall or a bump of something else. Even with that concoction, I would still fall asleep in the classroom. I also tried my hardest to live the virtues that I was raised to have...the virtues I had before drugs destroyed them. I still had a conscience, but the urge to hustle for the drugs that I desired overpowered my conscience.

My metaphorical "abusers" had me dependent, mindless, and living my life purely for the "abuser." That metaphorical abuser was me, it was my ego, and it was the animated figure that I admired so much. I knew I needed to change my ways and kill off this egotistical addicted bastard that I'd become. I knew I was in drastic need of intervention, but the way it happened was extremely tragic and unexpected. Remember when I gave the three places drugs will lead you? A graveyard, an ICU unit, or behind bars are your three choices in the quitting ultimatum. Now it is time to find out where my metaphorical "abuser" led me after that final drug binge. The drug binge that ended with a toxicology report that consisted of benzodiazepines, cocaine, marijuana, methamphetamines, amphetamines, opium, and barbiturates...not to mention the LSD that couldn't be detected.

The weekend had passed, my roommates had returned, and I had been up on an extensive drug binge since Friday. It was now Monday and my body was lagging, my brain was not functioning correctly, and I was sure to collapse at any given moment. I was barely able to keep my eyes open, but I had to turn in that criminal justice project that was due by 8:00 a.m. I needed more substances in order to physically make that possible. With that said, I consumed another 120 mg of Vyvanse in order to regain my awareness, mobility skills, and the basic daily functions needed to make it through my academics.

I finally became somewhat coherent at 7:50 a.m., once the Vyvanse had kicked in. I got off the couch as if I was awakening from the dead, and anxiously rummaged through the apartment looking for Colton's longboard. I usually walked to class, but I needed something faster than my feet so I would not be late for class. My vision was distorted, my mobile abilities were tarnished, and I had no idea how I was going to get through the day. Knowing that I desperately needed sleep, I decided I would only go to my first class, then come back to the apartment and finally catch up on some rest. I found his longboard, sprinted out the door, and pushed as fast as possible to my first class. I was making great time.

After flying through several blocks, I approached the street closest to the university. This street consisted of a fairly steep hill that ended right at the main building of the university. My longboard's front wheel made contact with a rock at the end of the steep hill. The longboard came to a screeching halt, throwing me off it head first. My body was banged up, bruised, and bloody. I got back on the longboard and finished the journey to the classroom in agonizing pain. It seemed my body would never recover from the fall. My head was pounding and my entire body ached as I walked into the building ten minutes late.

Everyone stared at the scratches, scrapes, and blood that blanketed my body. I looked like a zombie walking into the room. I turned in the paper and apologized for being late as everyone stared at me, speechless. It was apparent to the entire classroom that I was not capable of withstanding an entire class period. With that said, my professor excused me from the rest of the class period. She accepted my project, and with overwhelming sympathy she told me to get some rest, not knowing it would be my last day attending the class. I handed her the paper with my bloody hand and left the university's premises.

When I returned to the apartment, all of the goons were already awake. It was 9:00 a.m. and they were already drinking. The fact that they were drinking as soon as they woke up wasn't a surprise, but the fact that they were up before two in the afternoon was. The group was hanging outside grilling breakfast. Full of life, they informed me of the plan for the day. They decided we were going to grill all day. Alex had a surplus of venison he had hunted over spring break that was taking up our entire freezer. He woke everyone up in the house and explained how he wanted to cook and drink all day between classes for his birthday. I forgot it was his birthday, and I decided I couldn't deny his birthday request. I agreed that I would participate in grilling out for the day, even though I was completely aware I should have spent the remainder of the day catching up on rest.

We were drinking all day and my body was truly suffering from it. We had a keg, liquor, cases, marijuana, MDMA, and cocaine that we were consuming throughout the entire day. Rachel also had some rocks, but we were attempting to keep it away from Jayden. By mid-day, we brought out the lacrosse equipment to play catch. We were not completely physically engaged, but the minimal activity was starting to take a toll on my body. It started to make my heart ache horribly. My heart was undergoing unbearable pain, but I completely ignored it, figuring it was just heartburn from drinking too fast. The ache was present for about an hour when I finally realized I needed to go back upstairs and lie down.

When I went to go lie down, I realized I was restless. My eyes were shut, I was yawning in desperate need of sleep, but I just lay there watching the inside of my eyelids due to the substances that made it impossible to fall asleep. It was unbelievable that the drugs that I consumed made it so I was incapable of sleeping, even after being up for four days. My mind said sleep, but the chemical alterations denied my brain's request. I was on the couch with my eyes sealed for about an hour when Justin came up from the cookout downstairs. I opened my eyes to see who it was. I realized there was no way I could sleep so I might as well engage in the festivities.

He'd brought a handle of vodka with him, and jokingly stated he needed my help drinking it. He made up a challenge for the two of us to finish the half-gallon in just one hour, and we did just that. Like fiends, my friend and I split the mass amount of alcohol, each having a quarter gallon. When we were about halfway through with the bottle, Rachel barged in with exciting news. "I found LSD!!!!" she exclaimed. She had never done LSD before, but she knew I loved it dearly. I would consistently tell the group how I'd rather have it than any other drug. I had been without my poison of choice for nearly three months, and I relapsed with my metaphorical "abuser" happily. I knew I was going to take the LSD as soon as possible, regardless of how badly I needed sleep.

We were warned that the LSD was potent, and to start with a single tab. This was an accurate suggestion that the dealer gave us, but for an addict this is impossible. We seem to typically ignore safety, moderation, and suggestions as addicted individuals. I had decided I would start with three. I was excited, but I knew if I didn't get rest something terrible was bound to happen from sleep deprivation. I was in the great debate of more drugs or sleep. As usual, the drugs won the debate. I agreed that I would do three hits of acid. I figured I would not do as much as I was used to, therefore I would be okay. Merely using justification once again for my addiction. The plan was I would trip, meaning I would have been up for almost five days, and then fall asleep through that Tuesday, making this my last binge ever.

I told Jayden I was going to quit everything. I told him I knew where my life was going, and how I would not be capable of stopping it if I didn't quit immediately. I already was at this point, but I did not consciously know that. Anyway, he agreed and suggested we do it together, just like we'd started together. The irony in this is the fact that we always claimed that we would be done with everything after "this one last time." We had been saying that since the get-go, since the time we'd tried ecstasy nearly four years prior. Addicts typically have many "one last times," and we had the biggest collection of anyone. Regardless of the array of previous attempts, I told him I truly needed this…it had to happen before something terrible took place.

We agreed that we would sell all of our paraphernalia, scales, and narcotic-related equipment to assure us that we were serious about quitting. We figured that would be a big step in the right direction. We sold all of our glass pieces, our scales, our grinders, and anything else that had to do with drugs. We decided we would use this money for the LSD, and after that we would stay accountable to one another, being done forever. We sold everything extremely cheap to Colton's friend to "show" how little we cared about drugs. We obtained a little over two hundred dollars, and with the two hundred dollars we purchased enough acid to provide for the entire group.

The inventory that we had could have been sold for at least five times the amount that we sold it for, but we were on a mission to prove how little drugs mattered to us. I was so motivated to kill this life and ego that I had called my little sister to inform her I was leaving my deviant addictions behind me after that night. She told my mother what I said, giving both of them a sense of relief. She was ecstatic that she would have her brother back, not knowing this very well could have been the last phone call she had with her older brother.

Around 7:00 p.m., I was wide awake due to the adrenaline from finally obtaining the LSD. I had wanted the LSD for months, and our parting "blow-out" from substances wouldn't be perfect without it. I had stashed four hits for myself. I took three of them immediately and stashed one away for later. Colton walked into the apartment as soon as we dropped the LSD. He asked if there was any left so he could take a look at it. I informed him I had one more, but I was saving it for later. He assured me that he just wanted to examine it and he had no interest in doing LSD that night.

When I handed him the tab of acid, he instantly threw it on his tongue and laughed. I instantly became outraged, threw him against the wall, and asked what the hell his problem was. I ran toward the wall I had pushed him against with my fist cocked back, but before I followed through with a full-blown punch, Jayden and Alex broke it up. Jayden and Colton took a breather outside to talk about what just happened. Colton explained how messed up I already was, the fact that I'd bought them for everyone else, how he was planning on paying me for it anyway, and how he sincerely felt it was not a big deal. Jayden played the role of the mediator, remaining unbiased, and he suggested he just go to a friend's until I calmed down. Colton agreed with Jayden and left the apartment to go hang out at his buddy's place from work. The same one who bought the paraphernalia from Jayden and me. He informed Jayden he would reside there for the night until my trip was over, not knowing the psychedelic adventure would come to a dramatic ending sooner than everyone thought.

After a couple hours, my psychedelic journey started going terribly wrong. It was spiraling out of control. It got to the point that I scared everyone out of my apartment except Jayden and Rachel. They knew someone had to monitor every move I made so I did not hurt myself, or anyone else. Alex had left to take a break from playing babysitter and go to his girlfriend's house. He let Jayden and Rachel know he would be right across the apartment hall. His girlfriend happened to live in the same complex. Justin thought I was simply having a "bad trip." It was his first time hallucinating, therefore he decided he had to leave before his first trip became as horrifying as mine was. Before the trip I'd convinced Rachel that LSD was the best drug in the world, but the first time she tried it, everything that happened contradicted that.

The abnormal behavior started with me ripping my shirt off. Jayden explained to Rachel it was no reason to freak out, because many bad trips have the side effect of ripping clothes off. This was an accurate statement, but it was just the start to my terrifying behavior. Once my clothes were off, I viciously started scratching my body to relieve the burning sensation under my skin. When it started everyone was only slightly worried, thinking it was just a normal "bad" trip. Jayden continued assuring everyone it would be okay, not knowing how bad things would ultimately become. With that said, everything started to get really bad, really quickly. Jayden didn't even know how to handle the next horrifying aspect of my trip. I started pacing back and forth, saying, "billions, billions, billions, billions, and billions" over and over again.

Jayden then took action. He figured if I saw how ridiculous I looked, I would calm down. With that said, Jayden decided he would show this video to me in the morning. In the beginning of the video he stated, "This is why we are stopping drugs, Brad." He videotaped me as I walked back and forth from the hallway, kitchen, into the bathroom, and then into Colton's room repeatedly. At this point, I was in only my boxers. Rachel and Jayden had followed me, since I was being so self-destructive. My heartbeat and head were throbbing, I was breathing heavily, and my blood flow was circulating viciously. They knew my trip had turned into something too insane to imagine and were prepared to call 9-1-1 if need be.

They both figured that if I was still able to stand and walk, it was not necessary to call the medics. This was a false assumption. Even though they believed an ambulance was not needed, they agreed that this trip was one that needed supervision that only a best friend and significant other could handle. From that point, they knew that they could not let me leave their sight, and furthermore, let me into everyone else's. Jayden and Rachel successfully accomplished this. No one knew what was truly happening in that apartment, until it took its plunging fall.

I had no control over my body, thoughts, or actions. I had opened the window and was looking down the side of the apartment. Jayden thought I was getting some fresh air. Seconds later I crept forward and put my left leg out of the bedroom window. After I had done that, it became apparent to Jayden that I was attempting to jump out the window. Jayden sprang off the couch and leaped to the window in order to save my life. Jayden grabbed my underwear and had to drag me back into the apartment, dislocating his arm while doing so. I sat back on the chair like nothing had happened, and when he asked what the hell was going through my mind I responded with "billions, billions, billions, and billions" once again. As a disclaimer, I am in no way, shape, or form suicidal, but I tried to jump out of my second-story window with no recollection of why.

Once that happened, Jayden knew he had to confine me. He quarantined me in Colton's room, hoping the trip would get better as he sat in front of me crying, but unfortunately for the both of us it continued to go south.

I finally was able to put words together, but words that Jayden would not want to hear or even want to be able to comprehend. I was holding my heart, screaming, "You don't want to know, you don't understand, you don't want to know," and followed that with my night's catchphrase of "billions, billions, billions, and billions." This incomprehensible phrase was me trying to explain that this trip consisted of countless trips I had taken prior throughout my life. The best way to describe what was happening is to reference it as "trip clips."

All of my trips essentially were slammed into one. These several trips that I experienced from prior trips to were originally seven or eight hours long. They now were condensed into "trip clips," lasting only thirty seconds. It was as if my life was flashing before my eyes, as if I were seeing that "moment before death" for hours. Many of my trips had a primary theme, with the most common theme being the animation figure. These trip clips were on a constant repeating cycle for hours and consistently happening more rapidly and vividly.

I was hallucinating that the Pillsbury Doughboy was coming, that I was a character in *Blue Mountain State*, that I was searching for the explanation of the "color red," that Jayden called the police and they were coming, and, most importantly, I was following the animation figure of me that was running back and forth through my apartment. The animation was showing me all of these trips for roughly thirty seconds at a time as we were pacing through my apartment. These trips were all on a repeating cycle of the "trip-clips" that were about to give me a heart attack. This was building anxiety and I just wanted it to stop. I was trying to explain that the animation had appeared and it was terrifying to Jayden. I couldn't explain the situation when Jayden desperately begged me to say something that made sense.

I finally found the ability to state, "We are not the only two here." Jayden started crying in confusion and fear of what I meant by that. He thought to himself that maybe I was seeing death, but he figured it was just the LSD and the environment that was starting to give him a bad trip. He kept calm and took a breath. Rachel, on the other hand, left after I stated that Jayden and I were not the only two there. She knew I was not talking about her being there, but what scared her was the fact that I was so under the influence I didn't even know she was at the apartment when she was sitting right behind Jayden. She told Jayden she needed to leave for a little bit and she would be back when I calmed down.

Jayden agreed, since he was the only person I was acknowledging anyway. She told Jayden to be careful. She told him she saw the most terrifying image in my eyes – the devil. That my eyes were a black hole of pure evil, and it appeared there was no soul underneath my pupils. She left. Now it was only Jayden and me there. After another thirty minutes of my racing heart, pacing feet, and delusional mind, the inevitable finally happened. I paced back and forth following this animation. It must have been a hallucination, but it was so real. I couldn't explain it with words at the time, but it was like I knew exactly what was getting ready to happen.

I knew I was getting ready to die, and the animation figure of myself, my ego, was the murderer. Whether this was pure hallucination, or a symbol from God himself, it was so surreal. It seemed that I was surely going to die trying to confront this animation figure. I saw death in that animation figure, in that apartment, right in front of my eyes, and it was coming directly for me. With that said, I continued pacing back and forth in our hallway, terrified, until the animation ran back into Colton's room. I ran into Colton's room and had a confrontation with death itself. The animation had disappeared, Jayden ran in behind me, and I dropped to the floor and instantly started shaking out of control. I was having a seizure, brutally convulsing on the floor, and vigorously fighting for life while dying in my friend's arms.

Jayden gently dropped my head off his arms and raced to find Alex. Sprinting across the hall, he busted their door wide open, screaming Alex's name as loud as he could. Thinking Jayden was just being belligerent, Alex's girlfriend informed him that Alex was already sleeping like a baby and he needed to go back to where he came from. His voice increased as he screamed at the top of his lungs, "BRAD IS DYING!!" She ran out of the apartment to see, thinking that Jayden was just hallucinating. She thought maybe I was sleeping and Jayden was hallucinating I'd died, because of how scared he'd been earlier in the night by the way I was acting. When she got there, she saw this was no hallucination. She had to bear the same horrific image that Jayden described. I was still convulsing and foaming at the mouth as if I were Regan from *The Exorcist*.

She gasped, grabbed her cell phone, and called an ambulance. She immediately hugged Jayden, apologized, and told him that he could sleep in her apartment once they got me out of the apartment and into the hands of doctors. The police, ambulance, and poison control unit were there in minutes. Squad cars and ambulance sirens were blaring in The Village parking lot as a ton of officials came sprinting upstairs to my apartment. They saw me collapsed on the floor, and started the process of stabbing me in the arms with an IV. It took several medics, officers, and other public figures to be able to restrain my convulsing body and race me to the closest hospital.

Jayden called my mother's cell phone after I had been taken from the apartment in an ambulance. Assuming it was my mother on the other end, he screamed, "Mama Shell, Mama Shell, Brad is gone, Brad is not with us! Mama Shell!" My mother was in the bathtub, meaning it was my sister who answered the phone. My sister broke out in tears and busted into my mother's bathroom, screaming "Mom!" repeatedly. My mother had never seen my sister so traumatized. She saw the phone, jumped out of the bathtub, and knew something had happened to me as soon as she heard Jayden on the other side of the phone. She proceeded to calm Jayden down by giving him the generic "It's okay, it will be okay," but Jayden knew nothing was okay. Poor Jayden was sitting in the room I had collapsed in. All there was left in the apartment was Jayden, my blood all over the floor from the trauma unit procedures, and pure sorrow. My mother calmed Jayden down as much as possible to figure out what had happened. He informed her that it was from a drug overdose, I had been struggling the entire night, and the night filled with hallucinations came to a fatal ending. My mother told Jayden to sit tight while she called the hospital for further information.

Jayden wrote a report for the police. He was forced to stay at the apartment while they figured out what had happened. When the police stepped out for a moment, Jayden made a few more calls. He called Justin to inform him that the police were there and if he was going to come back to do so with caution. He called Katlyn and requested that she wake my father up to deliver the terrible news. Finally, when the police completely left around 4:00 a.m., he called Rachel. Rachel came over immediately following Jayden's phone call. They mourned together, not knowing if they would ever talk to me again. The apartment, Radford, and possibly my existence would never be the same after that night, and they had no idea how they were going to cope with that fact. The two of them stayed up staring at the heavens for an answer. They were distraught, confused, and left in the dark, two individuals who would just be the start to an enormous ripple effect.

As I was in the ambulance, people were waking up in the peak hours of the night crying and mourning with one another. Stephanie from Kingsdale, Braden from home, everyone in Radford, and an array of my family and friends were up within a couple hours, attempting to contact one another. Katlyn was able to wake up my father, who then woke up Steven, who then woke up Ricky, and etc. While I was lying in the ambulance dying, I had no idea what ripple effect I had caused... People didn't go to work, some people attended a religious institution who typically wouldn't, and phone calls were being made to find out my status in the middle of the night. From California to Virginia, people were at a loss for words. Jayden immediately withdrew from school, called his parents to pick him up, told them what happened, and went back home, being certain that I was as good as dead... Everyone thought I was as good as dead, including the doctors.

I, on the other hand, felt nothing. I was unresponsive, and as we were driving to the hospital, the medics became convinced that I was not going to come out of that unconscious state. I arrived at the local Radford hospital and was rushed to the operating room. A nurse called my mother as soon as I arrived, and stayed on the phone with her the entire time they were trying to develop a plan of action to resuscitate me back to life. My father, however, was mentally and physically in shock. This was the first time he'd caught me doing drugs, or even had a suspicion about it. He didn't know what to do, therefore he shut down and did nothing for hours. With that said, my mom knew she had to stay strong.

She stayed on the telephone with the nurse while she was booking an airplane ticket out from California. She decided that she needed to book the ticket when the nurse told her that, more than likely, she was going to have to come say goodbye to her boy. All of my organs were failing. My kidneys were failing, my heart was far from stable, my lungs were bleeding, and my throat was brutally scarred. My mother frantically asked what the hospital's plan of action was after about twenty minutes of me being in the ICU with no answers. The nurse quickly came to the conclusion that the hospital I was currently at did not have the resources to save me. In so many words, they told my mother I would die in that hospital.

My mother became frantic after realizing that if action was not taken I would die at the Radford hospital. With that said, she demanded they get me on a helicopter. The nurse went into how expensive it would be since I did not have any insurance, and continued by explaining I would probably die either way. My mother's tone became filled with outrage, and she stated that if I was not on a helicopter to the regional ICU facility within the minute, there would be a lawsuit. With that said, within minutes I was being airlifted to Roanoke Regional Hospital. I was incubated while flying the ten minutes it took to arrive at the trauma unit. The hospital that was my last shot at life. It became apparent that I was unable to breathe on my own.

The helicopter descended on the hospital's landing pad. I was rushed and admitted into the ICU. Once I was resuscitated and placed on a respirator, they gave me all the medical necessities for airflow, because I obviously was unable to breathe without medical intervention. After the admission into the ICU, the tragedy was quickly turned over to Poison Control. Once it was in their hands, they gave me a drug screening to determine why I laid there lifeless. Once my toxicology report came back, the results were unbelievable. Literally, Poison Control could not comprehend how I had not died days before I was admitted to the hospital.

A toxicology screen refers to various tests to determine the type, and approximate amount, of legal and illegal drugs a person has taken. I had an array of toxins in this report, including: opiates, benzodiazepines, methamphetamines, cannabis, alcohol, barbiturates, cocaine, amphetamines, and certain metabolites. Many of the items on the report were showing a significant amount of consumption. An amount that many of the professionals had never seen. The team was witnessing the impossible. It became obvious that my chances of waking up were slim to none.

The numbers were so high that Poison Control did not have an antidote to counteract the drugs, and they were convinced I was trying to kill myself (which I was not). They came to the conclusion that my body could not take another substance, whether it was professionally administered or not. My body had reached its "chemical capacity." The only antidote for something of this magnitude was time itself. The poison control unit and the medical doctors that reviewed my case and condition both agreed that only time would determine whether I would live, and at that moment time was not on my side. The only thing the doctors, my family, and my friends could do was pray that God would give me a second chance. With that said, I lay on my deathbed to start the first day of my coma that was deemed impossible to recover from.

The first day, I was completely unresponsive. The medical staff was positive there was no chance of me becoming conscious. Jayden had made it back safely to Ridge Run with Mr. and Mrs. Powers, Rachel was on her way home to attend rehab, and my other amigos were finishing their semester. Alex was sent by the group to attempt a visit with me at the hospital, although they were telling people no over the phone. He would soon find out that they were denying access to anyone until my immediate family had arrived to grant the permission.

Unfortunately, no family had arrived yet to grant Alex's request. He was able to leave me a note that was placed next to my hospital bed. My father was struck and so distraught that he refused to appear at the hospital. My mother was waiting for the soonest possible flight, which was not for a couple days. She was doing her research while she awaited her scheduled flight, rummaging through my Facebook, cell phone records, and other communication tools that I had used. What she found almost gave her a heart attack. She found messages between me and friends, messages between me and drug dealers, and, to her surprise, the intimate conversations that I had with Rachel.

My mother's first move was to delete the incriminating messages that blanketed my inboxes before authorities were able to obtain a warrant for them. It didn't surprise her that I had such incriminating messages, but what did surprise her was the fact that I had a mistress. She had no idea that my relationship with Stephanie had recently ended. She immediately called Jayden and interrogated him about who Rachel was, what our relationship with her was, and how I had become so intimate with her, assuming I was still dating Stephanie. Keep in mind that nobody except for my roommates knew about my affair or the breakup, and nobody except my roommates would ever see me as the cheating type. I never was the cheating type until drugs controlled and corroded my brain. Jayden, out of anxiety, gave it all up to my mother. He told her I'd been involved in an affair, and had broken up with Stephanie out of guilt. He also told her that Rachel was the source of the LSD that ended my drug binge.

My mom dug deeper and obtained Rachel's number through my cell phone records. She called Rachel repeatedly, threatening her with physical harm, and bombarded her with questions. My mother continually called Rachel until she no longer responded to my mother's outrage. She made it clear to Rachel that if she was to try and make contact with me, charges would be filed and executed. My mother knew she would not have to deal with Rachel after that, but she had no idea if she should be the one to bear the horrible news to Stephanie.

With that said, my mother decided to not tell Stephanie anything until Stephanie was permitted to visit me in the hospital. Stephanie's request of course would be granted as soon as a parent was there to give permission. In regards to Rachel, she dropped off the face of the earth as a result of my mother's threats. Rachel was not the only person to drop off the face of the earth; I as well was on my way out of this world the first day of my coma. I was unable to breathe on my own. With my lungs and bladder bleeding, kidneys failing, throat in critical condition, and the rest of my organs progressively dying, I was sure to be a goner within days.

Day two of my coma was no different from the first. My body was in critical condition, the toxins had overpowered the necessary functions that are needed to live, and the medical staff thought we were just waiting for the inevitable. The inevitable cycle of death from an overdose. On the other side of the country, my mom was still in the process of trying to convince my dad to go to the hospital. He was still distraught, confused, and unsure of what to do. He proclaimed that all he could do was look to God, whether he was in Roanoke or Ridge Run. He explained to my mom that I wouldn't even know he was there, therefore he was not helping anything while simultaneously undergoing an unbearable amount of pain that would derive from actually having to view the tragedy. Ultimately, my stepmother was in his head, and she had my father completely convinced it was not worth it.

They were right in a sense. They couldn't do anything for me while I was in such critical condition. In fact, no one could do anything; time remained the only factor. I still remained completely unresponsive, my organs were still failing, and death still seemed to be inevitable. The medical staff also came to the conclusion that if I were lucky enough to live, I would not be the same. They were almost positive that if I were to pull through by the grace of God, I still had a significant chance of being completely braindead for the remainder of my life.

I remained unconscious as midnight struck on the third day of my coma. I lay there lifeless, but an EEG report confirmed activity. God's miracles seemed to start benefiting my critical condition, although the results were miniscule. The medical team believed that I might be able to wake up under the right medication and equipment. They knew I was not completely recovered, but they wanted to witness my reactions, brain strength, and test the ability of my body functioning independently. When they tried to wake me up, they realized they had made a terrible decision.

The drugs that I was under continued to have a negative effect on my brain, and this was almost four days after I had consumed them. I became extremely combative toward the medical staff. I swung my fists, kicked my legs, and shook my entire body till I had literally flipped myself off the hospital bed and hung from my IVs. I have no recollection of this happening, nor did I have any control over my body. Many of the professionals had never dealt with such a combative awakening. I was putting full force into violently shaking my entire body. I had sustained many self-inflicted injuries due to this combative awakening. My arm was blanketed by an enormous purple and black bruise from needles ripping out of my veins. This was a direct result of when I had flipped off the bed.

Even more bothersome, I had bitten through the respirator tube on my way down. Once they completely removed the respirator from my mouth, I continued biting as if the respirator were still there. This resulted in me biting completely through my tongue. My combative reaction continued until the staff was able to pin me to the bed with several tightened restraints covering my body. Reports state that the staff needed two doctors, two nurses, and additional assistance of two other hospital aides in order to restrain me to the bed. They decided they would keep me in a medically induced coma until someone that I was familiar with was present to assure me that everything was okay. They concluded that my combative actions were caused by the drugs and the shock of my sudden awakening.

My father finally arrived and my mother was on her flight during the fourth day I resided in the intensive care unit of Roanoke's hospital. When my father entered the hospital, he nervously sat in the waiting room while they set up everything needed for the second attempt of bringing the medically induced coma to an end. They informed my father of the events that had taken place the day before. They gave him the professional opinion that I had a better chance of having a successful awakening if he was by my side to assure me of my safety.

With that said, my father and the medical staff entered the intensive care unit. My father walked by the bed and grabbed my lifeless hand. They executed the operations necessary to slowly wake me up. I was struggling as I attempted to open my eyes, but they rolled back shut seconds after. I gripped my father's hand extremely tightly, giving him more hope than he'd had all week. My father then gasped in relief, started crying, and said softly, "I'm here, Brad. I'm here." He continued by telling me that my mother was currently on a flight to Roanoke.

I still could not verbally respond, which scared my father that I was in a brain-damaged state as the doctors predicted, but with all the strength I had I started to shake my head no. This wasn't the reaction my father was hoping for, but it nonetheless gave him hope that I would eventually recover. My mother was at the hospital a couple hours after I had been declared conscious. When she got there I was still unable to speak, but the doctors had delightful news. My organs were starting to function again, slowly but surely. A miracle was starting to take place in Roanoke's hospital. Every dark night becomes a brighter day, but in my case a long day of good news was followed by a longer night of bad news.

Finally, there were words that escaped my mouth. I spoke my first words: "My baby, I want my baby." My mother could only assume I meant Stephanie, and therefore she granted permission for Stephanie to come visit me. Once I felt the soft touch of my now ex-girlfriend, I said, "Rachel, you came." Stephanie was shocked, and I was clearly hallucinating. I thought she truly was Rachel, even after she left the ICU. All I could think was, why would Rachel leave me? After the awkward encounter, my mother comforted Stephanie and explained who Rachel was to my father.

This was the first time either of them knew about my reasoning for breaking up with Stephanie or the affair. Stephanie didn't believe it. We were broken up at the time, although she thought it was a simple break. She was finally convinced that the breakup was due to daily stressors, and she figured that we would eventually get back together. She had a hunch it was for someone else, but she didn't know that Rachel and I were intimate before I officially ended the relationship. She was outraged, fooled, and completely hated me after she found out the breakup was to end the affair. She felt like an idiot, and saw me as a bigger idiot for choosing another girl with such terrible attributes.

My father and mother were both unaware that Stephanie and I had broken up. I did not want them knowing that I broke up with her, since it would lead to further questions I did not want to answer. I knew neither of my parents would approve of Rachel. My parents were disappointed, confused, and did not see why I would blatantly choose such a person to be in a relationship with. Stephanie was rightfully angry the night she was allowed to see me, and returned to Kingsdale shortly after this traumatic experience. In conclusion, the fourth day of my coma was a mixture of hope and hopelessness, love and hatred, and miracles and disasters. It was a night that consisted of the first time I had independence with my breathing, my consciousness, and my thought. It was also a night that my deceptive actions, the magnitude of my addiction, and all my hellish past hit the fan.

Five days later and hundreds of thousands of dollars in medical debt, I woke up like a normal human being, except for the catheter and respirator. I was not violent and I looked aware. The medical staff and my family were in disbelief. I seemed to be 100% coherent. The medical staff asked me extremely simple questions, such as who the president was, how old I was, where I went to school, and what my major was. I answered them without hesitation, and they looked at my parents to ensure those were the correct answers. They both nodded with approval. They then asked me where I was, and I answered a hospital. They asked me what had happened, and I stated I must have had a bad hangover…

After they informed me I'd overdosed, I sat up, the devastating reality hitting me. I noticed that I was in no basic hospital unit. I looked around the room and saw several doctors, psychiatrists, and my parents all staring at me in disbelief. My heart dropped, and they continued by asking what day it was. I responded Tuesday, and I was completely off. Although I'd answered the question wrong, the interviewer was intrigued as to why I answered the way I did. The interviewing doctor continued by asking why I thought it was Tuesday, and I answered, "Well…I remember doing LSD last night, and last night was Monday." He was in disbelief that I remembered what ended my drug binge, and, furthermore, that I remembered what day I overdosed. He took a deep breath and stated that it was Saturday evening, and the entire medical staff was convinced for days that my life was going to be taken from me. My eyes instantly became tearful and I couldn't believe what was happening.

I was determined to start functioning for myself. Within the hour, I walked through the ICU unit as if that were the best thing in the world. The only thing better than walking was the fact that I could actually use the restroom on my own. Long story short, all the professionals agreed I had made a recovery that could only be described as a miracle. I insisted that they let me leave, but they explained how I still needed medications, such as steroids and anti-psychotics, to ensure a safe recovery. They informed my parents that there was still a potential for side effects such as nausea, suicidal thoughts, and hallucinations. They were absolutely right about that. It only lasted for about twenty-four hours, but I hallucinated that Rachel was in the building. They would not let her in, and because of that I was unstrapping myself to go to the apartment to see her. I would imagine that I would run back to the hospital before the nurses noticed I was gone. When I snapped out of the final hallucinations I figured they were dreams, but after the fact the nurses said my "dream" description made sense, considering the documented hallucinations that I'd had while I was declared conscious.

By the sixth day that I spent in the intensive care unit, my hallucinations had ended. I was completely competent, and unfortunately it was the first day I comprehended every aspect of the tragedy. I finally felt the full effect of my mistakes. I internalized the ripple effect, the self-inflicted damage, and most of all the array of people I hurt. Jayden was the first person that came to mind when I thought about all of this. Ironically, Jayden was told if I were to wake up I probably would not remember who he was. With that said, I called Jayden and apologized for everything as I simultaneously thanked him. I was a ball of emotion as soon as he answered the phone call. He claimed that it was okay, and he was just happy I was alive.

The only business we had left at the hospital was an extensive psych evaluation. The results were not surprising. They concluded that I was not suicidal, although I had terrible coping issues that I had to work on. That was a no-brainer. All addicts have coping issues. The psychiatric team informed me that it seemed my main stressors were my mother's cancer and the fact that I lived so far from my family. They continued by explaining how critical it was that I went to rehabilitation in order to improve my coping skills and continue my road to recovery. They also suggested a sobriety animal or a new hobby to relieve the urges of drug abuse. The conclusion of the evaluation was I did not need antidepressants as of now, but I had to learn to cope with my daily stressors.

After the evaluation, I left the hospital, thanking every doctor and nurse on the way out. I received over 500,000-dollars in medical debt, but more importantly I received the priceless second chance.

That bill of over half a million dollars was reduced to 16,800 dollars. In fact, that was only for the third-party helicopter. My medical bills were waived, my body was functioning, and I could not describe the miracle that was given to me in any way except as a second chance.

We pulled out of the hospital and went to Walmart to get me some clothes that I could change into. I was in pajama bottoms and a T-shirt that my mother had brought in when she got to Roanoke. We walked through the checkout line that was being operated by an elderly cashier. She was sweet and seemed to have a lot of interest in me. It was strange, and I felt a supernatural phenomenon happening as she was gazing into my eyes. She didn't welcome us with the generic "hey, how are you" that most cashiers do, but instead commented on the fact that I was helping my mother load the groceries. I smiled at her and nodded my head. She then suddenly asked if I was okay, and I nodded with a pleasant smile again with no verbal response. Somehow she knew I'd been in the hospital even though I had already taken off my band stating that I was admitted, and she asked, "Son, you just left the hospital, why is that?"

My cheeks blushed. I took a deep breath, and I faced the reality, responding with, "I overdosed on drugs and almost lost my life."

She seemed as if she was ignoring my statement and commented on the "older gentleman standing behind me." I turned my neck, but saw no one there. She then looked my mother in the eye and stated, "It is your father." My mother responded by stating that was impossible; her father had been dead for years. The cashier smiled and stated, "I know." She then looked at me and continued, "You didn't almost die, son. You have died twice before." What this meant, I am not exactly sure...

All I knew was someone was looking after me from the heavens, and I received a second chance. The second chance to help addicts who are being controlled by their metaphorical abuser. The second chance to save the individuals who have a collar around their neck. The second chance to explain the process of addiction by an addict for the addict. The second chance to share my journey.

The second chance to say...
"Hi, my name is Brad, and I am a RECOVERING drug addict."

VI.
Adding Addiction

"THE TRADITIONAL OUTLOOK WITH A TWIST"

THE DAY THAT I RETURNED to Ridge Run, I did what any addict seeking help would do. The day after I arrived I enrolled in Narcotics Anonymous, Alcoholics Anonymous, and one-on-one counseling sessions. Although many of the AA and NA tactics are outdated, they are still extremely resourceful. When an addict reaches the point of rock bottom, it is hard for them to relate to friends and family members. With that said, both AA and NA are extremely helpful in finding empathy from normal human beings who somehow found themselves in the same situation you are in, and more importantly, many of them are recovering as living proof that sobriety is possible.

The process of recovery typically involves the twelve-step program, and for me this was a great base to start with. Obviously step one, admitting, is absolutely necessary. Or step six, patch up grievances, is an extremely helpful tool to receive forgiveness from your loved ones and yourself. I did see some problems with the program as a whole. One issue with this type of program is the fact that some participants see this as "story time." Some saw it as an hour session that contained insight, experiences, and traumatic events that your peers would share with the rest of the groups. Do not get me wrong, this is an extraordinary tool, but I do not believe it can be the primary assistance to recovery, and several recovering addicts use the twelve steps as their primary "medicine." It neglects how they became an addict, and it is impossible to fix a problem if you do not truly understand where it blossomed from. This is a huge factor in our country's low recovery rate and high recidivism rate.

This is insufficient simply because there is not enough collaboration on recovering tactics; instead you hear people's stories that you can relate to. Rarely in AA and NA did I hear how people were recovering, although I heard an array of stories about how people hit rock bottom. The primary purpose of these programs is to obtain support, but a solution this simple cannot solve such a complex problem as addiction. Being able to relate to a support group cannot singlehandedly help save an addict. This is precisely why people can go to AA, remain in the program, follow the twelve steps, and can also find themselves reliving their nightmare of addiction.

Remember, addiction is a sickness. Is a cancer patient going to rely on a support group to cure the illness? No, of course not, so why would an addict? With that said, I see AA as similar to a cancer support group. The support group was established to realize you have support and you are not alone, but it is not there to cure or regress the disease. This is how I see AA, NA, and other programs of this nature.

I used another resource that many recovering addicts use as well: a counselor. I started seeing a one-on-one psychiatrist to help me find the root of my coping and polysubstance abuse issues. The original counselor I was seeing was very conservative, religious, and dedicating to helping people. Overall, he was a wonderful professional and a delightful human being with good intentions and morals. He was an elderly Hebrew gentleman. I'm Jewish by affiliation, although it was not a huge part of my daily ritual. My father believed he'd found the right counselor due to the fact that the professional worked with a temple that my father was associated with. On the other hand, I found the psychiatric session problematic, and I was the one that needed recovery...

If you are a parent, make sure the counselor is right for your child, not you. Refer to *Good Will Hunting* and how Will (Matt Damon) acted toward a psychiatrist that he could not relate to. Although they were prestigious, had achieved an admirable amount of education, and had helped a plethora of other individuals, something was problematic. He took therapy as a complete joke until he found the psychiatrist played by Robin Williams. This fictional movie truly makes my point in regards to therapy and the relationship required by the client and the addict to be successful. It is extremely hard for an addict to wrap their mind around the fact that people think talking to some older high-class gentleman is going to make the addict "normal" again. The addict needs to find someone that is compatible with them specifically, and if they do not find that the counseling sessions will be pointless.

My personal dilemma with my first psychiatrist was that the psychiatric sessions consisted purely of religion, as many addiction programs do. The primary base of the doctor's solution was that the addict needed to place his fate in the hands of God. The addict had to turn away from drugs, and the only way that was possible was to place their fate into God. I am not an atheist, but I believe that YOU have to overcome addiction, YOU are to thank for your success, YOU are to blame for your failure, and ultimately God gives YOU the free will to determine a recovery or a relapse. It was YOU who got yourself into drugs, slightly accompanied by psycho-sociological factors, and recovery will depend on YOU and an improved psycho-sociological environment. My opinion was, and still is, that God only helps those who help themselves.

If you have a strong religious affiliation, a program like the one above will potentially bring you the best results. But if you are not religious, you will not have the common ground that the entire program is based on. With that said, you are lying to the program and yourself. I expressed my view to the counselor, and he looked at me with disapproval. This doctor could not disagree with me more, and this was a sign that his services were not right for me. His program was too dependent on God's grace, making it impossible for me to relate. It was also apparent to me that he had never dealt with addiction. I needed a cure whose base was self-empowerment. This was crucial, and something every addict needs back – the ability of self-empowering. These two opposite attributes (religion and self-empowerment) of curing addiction are not right or wrong, but they definitely are not aligned or compatible with one another.

The twelve steps can involve anywhere from a little to a lot of religious affiliation; it varies. This is because each AA that is configured can range in gender, age, background, affiliation, severity of addiction, etc. I believe the twelve steps is the best support group; therefore, if you're not religious, I would still stick through your agonizing pain of listening to the aspects of the program you do not believe in. Take out what you do believe, but do not disrespect the sections that help other people. If you are like me and believe God only helps those who help themselves, or believe in this "self-empowerment" theory, then listen to the sections that disagree. You can listen to a contradicting belief, but if it doesn't sit right with you then disregard it.

You are there for support, opinions, options, and empathy – not to cure the addiction. Let's use the cancer support group for another metaphor. In this cancer support group *(compared to AA)*, a woman gives her reasoning on why she chose radiation rather than chemotherapy *(compare to religion vs. self-empowerment)*. Is the man who decided to do chemo going to disassociate from the support group because they disagreed? Highly doubtful. He will more than likely determine why the woman decided differently than he did, internalize the information, and optimize his knowledge and compassion through this support group. It should be the same principle for twelve-step groups.

On the other hand, I believe the opposite about one-on-one counseling. You need to find someone who shares the same religion, values, and thought process (besides being an addict, that is). The counselor should share these foundational values, since it is only you two in the group. His wisdom is the only wisdom you hear, and he hears only the insight you share with him. This is why you will optimize results if there is a strong common ground from the get-go.

I hope this sheds some light on some of the traditional and most common forms of recovery. These attributes alone are overlooked a lot of the time. They are viewed as pass/fail, or works/doesn't. They are the same black-and-white attitudes that most people have toward addiction in its entirety. Addicts and loved ones should really put a considerable amount of time into developing a strategy when it comes to AA/NA and counseling. Use AA/NA as the support group, and use the counseling as a form of medicine. The AA/NA is your "cancer support group" for empathy, and the counseling is one form of "chemo or radiation" to start your recovery process.

There is one more "cure" for addiction that has never seen the light, and my last chapter will explain this "chemo" that could cure all addicts across the globe. Beautiful wives, husbands, sons, daughters, friends, etc. have added an addict to the family dynamic. Their new addictive persona has now intruded into the family's daily routine...so now it is time to fight fire with absolutely nothing, simply adding the addiction. Adding the addictive personality to everyday life. This will not make an addict ordinary again, or the same person they once were... In fact, this theory has the potential to make an addict extraordinary.

"THE SECOND CHANCE"

I SINCERELY BELIEVE, AND hope this to be true, that I have explained addiction in a light that you cannot receive from a graduate-school textbook. I needed to find a book like this one that shed a light on recovery besides a traumatic story, a PhD, and a religious base. I couldn't find one, so I made one. I believe I was given a second chance to bring these abstract outlooks and alternative solutions, and reveal this light to the world that has never been seen in regards to addiction and the recovery process. Once again, I believe that the addict will learn the most from a recovered addict rather than an individual who obtained a piece of paper after eight years but has not dealt with addiction on a firsthand basis. I am not putting down the dedicated student who received a PhD in psychology, social work, etc. In fact, I believe a PhD who has experienced addiction on a firsthand basis is ideal.

Another ideal role model is a sponsor. The sponsor program is based off the theory of learning from an addict who has been in recovery for a significant amount of time, sometimes ten, twenty, thirty years... The idea is to be professionally evaluated and have a recovering addict in the program to mentor and navigate a new addict through a recovery process. The counselor I found to assist me in recovering was a mixture of those two resources. He was a recovered addict, he was my sponsor, and additionally he had a masters in counseling. Even though he hadn't reached the same educational "qualifications" my prior counselor had, he was a lot more impactful. Do not use ratings, education, or qualifications as your only deciding factors in choosing a psychiatrist.

His name was Michael. In my first session with Mr. Michael, he admitted that he was an alcoholic until he was in his mid-forties.

When he was forty-five, he claimed to be given a "second chance" just like me. He used this opportunity to go to school, with the ultimate goal of saving addicts through counseling. He was the first remarkable resource for my recovery, and he became a very influential person in my life. My belief that addiction is a long, complex process that needs an abstract solution, and ultimately that addiction and recovery varies with every case, came from him. With that said, our first approach was focusing on a hobby, and in turn, becoming addicted to a beneficial hobby rather than chemicals. I found a term, a theory, and a plan based on this. I like to call it ADDING ADDICTION.

I had two predominant hobbies that took over the state of my recovery: lifting weights and lyrical poetry. Lyrical poetry could be considered rap, but with the negative connotations that rap has accumulated over the years I want to clearly explain what my hobby of rapping truly is. I rap about life events, how I view them, give clarification on my thoughts, and accompany those thoughts with word play. Firstly, I enjoyed telling my side of things through music. Secondly, I was fascinated with manipulating the English language to force words to rhyme; it became an obsession. These are two reasons why I love a recovering drug addict you probably have heard of: Eminem! I spoke, and listened to, these lyrical words of wisdom to help cope with what had happened. I used rap as an accessory, or outlet, to recover from drug addiction.

Lifting weights was the second hobby that truly grasped my attention to the point that it was an addiction. It gave me adrenaline to replace the rush sensation that I had once craved from drugs such as MDMA and cocaine. When I lifted weights, it felt as if I was lifting stress out of my body. I highly recommend intertwining physical workouts with a recovery program… "The runner's high." It is scientifically proven that there is a connection between physically challenging the body and challenging the body mentally. Therefore, you can use physical workouts in order to work out mentally. This is an extremely powerful tool to recover from addiction. I focused all of my spare time on these two hobbies, and sure enough they were replacing my addiction to drugs. It wasn't easy, but it relieved the anxiety of sobriety.

I was adding to my addiction-craving mind. The addict is almost addicted to addiction in itself. The idea here is not to suppress your addiction tendencies completely, but instead replace the addictive tendencies with something beneficial. For example, Mark Cuban is addicted to success, Tom Hanks is addicted to acting, Will Ferrell is addicted to comedy, and Oprah is addicted to helping people. These individuals are obsessive about the things they do. This is why they became one of the best in the world at what they do. Debatably, obsession and addiction could be used interchangeably. Addiction does come with the connotation of a "need" or a chemical dependency, but the overwhelming urge is an attribute in both obsession and addiction. Essentially, these words mean putting your all into the things you do, whether it be an activity or a substance. These words mean desperately wanting something, almost to the point that it could arguably be a "need."

Regardless of what an individual may believe, you cannot argue that addicts are not obsessive, or don't have obsessive tendencies. They are typically obsessive about their self, significant others, and the drug itself to the point that it endangers them. Unfortunately, drug addicts become in love with the alterations and chemical reactions in their brain rather than something that is beneficial, like the public figures I mentioned above. This is unfortunate for two reasons. Firstly, the addiction a drug addict develops is clearly and immensely unhealthy. Secondly, the chemical addiction intertwines with the predisposition of the biologically inherited addictive personality to make the cohesive bond that is incredibly difficult to overcome.

When individuals are recovering they try to kill their addictive personality. Unfortunately, the harsh reality is that it will be there forever. Sociologically and biologically, it is so ingrained that it is nearly impossible to suppress. An addict is an addict for life, which is why the term recovered/recovering addict is used over a term such as "ex-addict" or "former addict." In fact, I've met people in AA and

NA who have been clean for twenty-plus years but still state, "My name is [insert name here], and I am an addict." With that said, once an addict, always an addict. However, if the addict can control their addiction, not attempt to diminish it, they have the opportunity to use it toward something beneficial. So beneficial that not only can they change their life, but they can change the world. They can recover from the chemical dependencies and use the addictive mindset to do something extraordinary.

I started working with this theory of "adding my addiction," and it did wonders for my recovery and moving toward my ideal self. I started working out every day for hours. I would research workouts, diets, and routines every night. With the remainder of my free time I wrote lyrics, listened to inspiring artists, recorded music, and even started to build enough confidence to release my own work. It got to the point where I released a new piece of work almost every other day. It quickly became routinized, an obsession, a new addiction.

I can even use this book itself as an example, and it has by far been my biggest addiction. If someone without the addictive personality wants to help people with addiction, they may talk to friends, give advice, or even help a stranger. Someone with the addictive personality, whether they were addicted to drugs or not, will give speeches at schools, get their PhD, or even write a book on addiction to help individuals who have been struck by drug abuse. They will do anything to get what they want. It is the obsession, the addiction, the same personality that is so discouraged in drug addicts, and it is working toward helping society.

The idea of replacing your addiction rather than trying to minimize your addictive personality is what my success has come from. These are the grounds on which I developed the theory of Adding Addiction(s). Essentially, use your God-given trait of obsession for good. Essentially, you can benefit from the addictive personality. Yes, I said it – YOU CAN BENEFIT FROM THE ADDICTIVE PERSONALITY. You cannot benefit from being addicted to drugs, but no one could argue that you cannot benefit the greater good by being addicted to work ethic, love, or generosity. You should continue to stay up restlessly, do anything for what you desire, and let your addiction control your life, but instead of letting your addiction be drugs, make it something beneficial. Take something that will improve your way of life and then become helplessly addicted to it. If you already have the inherited advantage, why not use it? Everyone claims that addiction is a terrible predisposition, but does it have to be? Once I started to take my own advice on "adding my addiction," every aspect of my life truly started looking up for me.

With that said, I decided that school was going to be my next addiction. I was ready. I figured I would just continue to add beneficial addictions while I simultaneously was diminishing my urge for drugs. This continued to work wonders, but just like they say in NA, "It only works if you work it." Similar to NA, you also need a support group to make this work. My father was not convinced that I was ready to go back to college. He believed I needed to be under his supervision, and the few months that I was home was not enough to assure him that I was truly a recovering addict. He firmly believed that, and rightfully so.

To reiterate, you need to find someone that is as obsessed with your new, and beneficial, addiction to support you through the transition. I had this support network from the brothers of Pi Lambda Phi at Radford University. Several of their brothers were there for me, supported my recovery, and would consistently ask me what I was doing to benefit my life. They questioned me on my next moves, when/if I would be returning to school, and became a secondary parent figure to ensure that I was attending my recovery meetings regularly.

After adding to my addiction with the gym, work, writing, and health, I decided it was time to add the addiction to my educational goals. After my conversations with the brothers of Pi Lambda Phi, my urge to improve myself, and a lot of contemplation, I decided that I needed to go back to school. I wanted to go back that following fall. I did not want to delay the process by going to a community college part time, or use the mindset of "there is always next semester." I was confident that my theory of Adding Addiction would work even though I'd only been implementing it for a short duration. Regardless, I was determined to go back to Radford University, join Pi Lambda Phi, and finish what I started – THE RIGHT WAY. I was going back to Radford and adding additional, beneficial addictions to reach my ideal self. That is what I truly desired, and that is exactly what I did.

This was my opportunity to put my money where my mouth was, to prove that Adding Addiction can really work. Entering school was not easy, but "not being easy" never deterred me from what I wanted, especially in my past addiction with obtaining drugs. I would relentlessly search, call, and find solutions to the answer "no" when I wanted drugs. With that said, I would not let anything hinder my chances of getting what I want. "Why should it now?" I thought to myself. It is the same attributes and principles of that incredible drive to capture what I wanted now as it was before. I had a plethora of requirements to fulfill just to be re-admitted to the university, including but not limited to: meetings with the dean, weekly counseling sessions, and an increased GPA requirement to remain enrolled. Long story short, nothing was in my favor to ensure I was in good standing with the university…one mess-up and I was gone for life.

I met with the dean for the first time days before school started. The meeting was delightful. The dean showed compassion, empathy, but also held a firm tone to reinforce the seriousness of my requirements to continue my enrollment at Radford University. We discussed my summer progress regarding recovery, my upcoming semester of academia, and potential opportunities and resources to relieve the challenge of overcoming substances. The dean started with generic advice in regards to studying, coping skills, and giving me contact information for various resources on campus. She then went into more specifics regarding my personal story and recovery. She had asked if there were any organizations that I had an interest in. I informed her that I was interested in Pi Lambda Phi, and I also held a particular interest in working at the local campus-owned Starbucks.

As school was approaching, I got in contact with the manager of the campus Starbucks, who was also a recovered addict. She was an incredible lady that could make any smile glisten while in her presence. She loved my story, my personality, and of course the fact that I had extensive experience with Starbucks. With that said, in no time at all I was hired! I let the dean know and she was ecstatic that I had accomplished on-campus employment. On the other hand, she wasn't too sure about the fraternity due to the stigma that the media has developed. I assured the dean how Pi Lambda Phi was different, and I knew it would be beneficial. She was indecisive about my intentions of joining, what challenges I might be faced with, and the ultimate outcome for me if I were to go through with joining Greek life.

Fall 2012 semester had started full force, and I was adapting to eighteen credit units, weekly counseling sessions, rush week, and my forty-plus-hour workweeks. I was successful in balancing these sectors of my life, something I couldn't fathom doing on drugs. I was preparing to have an additional sector on the scale I was attempting to balance, Pi Lambda Phi. I put forth a significant effort to interact with the brothers to assure them that I was on the right track. I'd left the hell of substances, and I was never going to turn back. It took a lot of convincing, and by the skin of my teeth I got the majority vote of "yes." I extended a bid to join Pi Lambda Phi as a new member of the fall 2012 class. I was excited, but I was also nervous that I would not be able to balance all of these sectors that rapidly merged into my life. I decided to contact my LCSW (licensed clinical social worker) and the dean of the university to look into resources to cope with the stressful semester that was ahead of me.

After extensive research, I believed that adding a furry friend would help me cope with stress that inevitably was developing. After a couple weeks of collaboration between my healthcare provider, the dean, and myself, I got approval to adopt a companion canine. My sobriety dog, Mac. When I got Mac, he was six weeks old. He is a beautiful American pitbull terrier, my pride and joy, and my best friend. He jumped straight into my arms, and I knew he was going to be an outlet of continuing my recovery. At that point in time, I knew that he was going to assist in keeping me clean. He was my dog, my responsibility, my companion, and my new addiction. I highly recommend an animal for recovering addicts. It helps give a sense of purpose, of responsibility, and is an opportunity for the addict to have a life form that is dependent on them. More importantly, depending on their sobriety.

Mac became an additional addiction, another aspect of Adding Addiction. I was addicted to my dog, his training, and my new title as a dog owner. I was determined to work with Mac every night. I started with simple commands such as sit, paw, lie down, roll over, and speak. As time went on he was able to give both paws, stay on command, move on command, and even developed the ability to understand specific words and movements that applied to no other dogs but him. When he was a few months old, people would say he was the most trained canine they had ever seen. In fact, other people were seeking my training advice and requesting I work with their dogs. Mac isn't just a dog; he is a contribution to my sobriety, the known dog around town, and my life companion.

As fall was coming to a close, I realized this whole Adding Addiction was working. I was a phenomenal new member, was still committed to my music, was exercising regularly, was working forty hours a week, and still was able to maintain straight As. As the year came to a close, I became a brother of Pi Lambda Phi, I had a perfect one-year-old puppy, maintained an impressive GPA, was appointed as a judicial board member and academic coordinator of my fraternity, impressed the hell out of my university and family, and most importantly, I was approaching my ideal self being sober for over a year.

My second year back at Radford University, I did not remain stagnant. I kept improving. An addict needs that recognition, and if they get it, their friends and family will watch them reach their full potential by adding their predisposed GIFT (their addictive personality). I came back as a Starbucks manager, a newly initiated brother of Pi Lambda Phi, a dean's-list student, and a newly admitted business major. I was paying my bills, not spending money on drugs. I was studying, not partying. I was training Mac, not having deceitful affairs. Essentially, my family and friends saw Brad back in action like they had never seen him before. They saw the kid that they were dying to take back from my "domestic abuser."

With that said, I continued my progress with Pi Lambda Phi by being elected vice president. I was now in a leadership position serving the men I had looked up to a year prior. I was officially an executive officer of Pi Lambda Phi. This happened rapidly, but with my resources I knew I could handle it. Vice President of Pi Lambda Phi entails being the president's right-hand man, but more importantly, the vice president is in charge of all new member activities. I had the privilege of sharing my story, my values, and what the fraternity meant to me with all of our new members. Consequently, I was awarded educator of the year. To put that comment in a tangible form, six of seven new members have served on a committee or executive board position after my education program.

I had the opportunity to teach the fraternity's values and morals, which include but are not limited to: being a gentleman, following your convictions, eliminating prejudices, respecting authority, and unity. Furthermore, I had the privilege to explain to them what it meant internally and externally that we were a "colony." We did not have our charter, which is a big deal in Greek life. If you recall, I mentioned what this means previously. Being a colony entails being scrutinized by the chapter's international headquarters. In other words, you are not in direct control of your chapter's operations; headquarters is. It is title that states, "That fraternity is small, new, and probably won't make it." This is what I stressed the most to the new members with the hope that one of them would be president one day and get the charter for previous presidents who were unable to successfully accomplish it due to the extensive requirements set out by our headquarters.

Ironically, when the semester ended (along with my term as VP) I was elected as the president. I had the opportunity to receive the charter myself. With my addictive personality I knew nothing was going to stop me from what I wanted, that charter for the fraternity I hold so dear. My addiction kicked in for Pi Lambda Phi, and from there I was unstoppable. With the help of my executive board, we had fixed our bank records from having no idea about accounting, recruited one of the largest classes of Greek life in the newest fraternity, developed service events that raised over thousands of dollars even though all odds were against us, developed study hours even though no one wanted to study on campus, and made a self-sufficient fraternity that no longer needed to be scrutinized by headquarters. Every brother documented ten hours of service, joined another on-campus organization, and fulfilled all of the other rigorous requirements given by our headquarters. Months later it was time to put together our chartering packet, a detailed document providing evidence of our successful year.

As the end of the year was approaching, the International Executive Council met with our executive director, national president, and Radford University's Greek life director to vote on Pi Lambda Phi at Radford University's charter. On May 20th, 2014, we received the call to tell us we received our charter! I was so proud and excited, and I even teared up a bit. As Drake's "We Made It" was blaring in the chapter house, brothers started piling in and screaming in joy. I walked into my room and thought of my progress, I petted Mac, and looked up to God and thanked him for instilling this thought of Adding Addiction into my head. In two years, I was a junior in the College of Business and Economics, a valuable employee at Starbucks, a self-supporting college student, the chartering president of Pi Lambda Phi at Radford University, and the sober Brad Korer I knew I could be. In fact, a better Brad Korer than I could have imagined.

Similar to new addictions in regards to drugs, a new healthy addiction doesn't necessarily have to replace the old healthy addictions. They merge, just like a coke addict can drink alcohol and become addicted to both. I continued with music, writing, and exercising. I simply added more addictions, such as the fraternity, my academics, my passion for developing business ideas and strategies, my canine, and the idea of reaching my potential.

Over the next summer I realized I needed to start increasing my drive. I had two huge reinforcements that I was on the right track. Firstly, we had our annual convention for our fraternity, where all chapters from the United States and Canada met in Raleigh, NC. I was able to go free of charge, due to a scholarship I was awarded for my achievements. The purpose of this convention was for leaders of the fraternity's chapters to collaborate on goals, strategies, and visions for the upcoming school year. It was also a morale booster with an annual ceremony where awards, recognition, and highlights of the year were disbursed.

Several awards were distributed to the chapter at Radford University. We were recognized and awarded for being chartered, won the most improved chapter award, were recognized for excellent recruitment, and I personally won Brother of the Year and nearly 2,000 dollars in scholarships for the duration of two consecutive terms as president. The purpose of explaining this is not to brag, but to convey that this is the moment I realized I was addicted. I was addicted to something that was for the greater good, but regardless, my addictive tendencies were present. I was up countless hours, wouldn't let anything or anyone stop me, and I was obsessive about my new addiction. These attributes are identical to drug addiction. This is a clear-cut example of how I used the theory of Adding Addiction to benefit my life, and the lives of others.

So where has Adding Addiction left me? I am still making music. I became a stakeholder with the global company of Audio Technica. I am on the advisory board for Pi Lambda Phi. I have completed my bachelor's programs. I am applying to M.B.A. programs. I am a current stakeholder of an E-commerce company, and my book, *Adding Addiction*, is making its way around the globe. Mac is three years old and healthier than ever. I've developed a strong sense of compassion and love, resulting in the best relationships I've ever had with my friends and family. Most of all, I've proved over the last four years that Adding Addiction works!

My accomplishments have made me proud of myself, but my addictive personality is always looking for more. Once again, my intentions are not to brag or boast. I wanted to give a brief example of how much Adding Addiction has benefited me in a few short years. I only can imagine how much this strategy can help others. My life would not be the same without this theory. In fact, I very well could have relapsed months after my tragedy. My purpose, my second chance, my destiny is all for one reason – to explain this theory. I want this to benefit addicts worldwide. You have a gift; use it.

It doesn't matter what the trait is; the gift comes from how you use it. For example, think about superheroes versus villains. The strength, power, and backgrounds are usually the same, but intentions are opposite. For a real life situation, take the military. Navy SEALs have a gift. They have self-discipline, intelligence, aim, strength, precision, bravery, and agility that are incredibly rare. You know who else had that? Nazi Germany. SEALs use these attributes they possess for a greater good, to protect our country. Is the country going to tell them to stop being so intelligent, strong, and brave because it opens up the door for them to be as dangerous as Hitler and Nazi Germany once was? Of course not. I know this is a touchy example that has two opposite extremes, but so is addiction…so why would you tell someone with an addictive personality to try and suppress their attributes? Persistence, a drive for what they want, obsession, and an abstract view of the world are all attributes of the most successful people in this world, but also characteristics of an addict.

"It doesn't matter what it is; it matters how you use it."

So the question you have to ask yourself is: how do you want to use the biological and sociological reality of the addictive personality? It truly is in your hands. The first step is to realize the non-inherited, or what I like to call secondary, corruptive attributes of an addict. This includes, but is not limited to: lying, deceiving, faulty comparison and justification, an egotistical mindset, carelessness, and, of course, your metaphoric "abuser(s)". The second step is deciphering the God-given traits of obsession, drive, and consistency. Finally, the third step is to put the primary, God-given attributes you possess into play to spawn something beneficial. Before you know it, you will be addicted to things in life that will make you prosper, that will give you a life of abundance, and will simultaneously keep your mind off drugs. This has worked for me; let it work for you.

This theory incorporates the personality traits that will not just turn an addict into an ordinary person, but also have the potential to turn the individual into an extraordinary human being. I beg that addicts around the world develop this strategy, this way of life. Allocate your addiction to something great, to something you love, and to something that is not destroying your life. Escape the grasp of your "domestic abuser" and find a healthy relationship to be addicted to (metaphorically speaking). I am becoming close to finally fulfilling my deepest addiction: helping addicts. I certainly became addicted to helping addicts, far more addicted than I was to drugs. I am not fulfilling the addiction by ending my book; it will be fulfilled once it is proven to work. FOR YOU. This is my purpose, my passion, my second chance to attempt to add addiction to something beneficial. I am Brad, the addict, and I am ADDING ADDICTION.

Printed in the USA
CPSIA information can be obtained
at www.ICGtesting.com
LVHW091458090923
757417LV00008B/276